Making Believe on Paper

Making Believe on Paper

Fiction Writing
with Young Children

TED DeMILLE

HEINEMANN
Portsmouth, NH

Heinemann
361 Hanover Street
Portsmouth, NH 03801–3912
www.heinemann.com

Offices and agents throughout the world

Library of Congress Cataloging-in-Publication Data
DeMille, Ted.
    Making believe on paper : fiction writing with young children / Ted DeMille—1st ed.
        p. cm.
    Includes bibliographical references and index.
    ISBN-13: 978-0-325-01748-8
    ISBN-10: 0-325-01748-4
    1. Creative writing (Elementary education). 2. Fiction—Study and teaching (Elementary). I. Title.
    LB1576.D37 2008
    372.62'3—dc22   2008028907

Editor: Harvey Daniels
Production: Patricia Adams
Typesetter: Pear Graphic Design
Cover design: Lisa Fowler
Manufacturing: Steve Bernier

Printed in the United States of America on acid-free paper
12 11 10 09 08 VP 1 2 3 4 5

This book is dedicated with love and respect
to my first reading mentors,
my departed mother and father,
Carole and Al DeMille,
and to my dear sister, Wendy.
A more loving, loyal, and generous sibling
no brother could ever find in this or any other world.

CONTENTS

*Y*ears ago, Nancy Martin—the late, pioneering, British researcher of student writing and learning—visited me and my husband for a summer weekend. At the time I was the director of a K–8 writing project at Boothbay Region Elementary and trying hard to follow in the mighty footsteps of Donald Graves, Lucy Calkins, and Susan Sowers—adopting the methods of writing workshop that emerged from their groundbreaking study at a New Hampshire elementary school. Nancy wanted to know all about it.

So we walked and talked our way down the road to the beach, then stretched out side by side on one of the flat slabs of rock revealed at low tide. I launched into a description of Boothbay's writing workshops—how children had time to write every day, conferences with the teacher about their drafts, encouragement to experience writing as a multiphase process, and their own choices of topics and audiences. About the last I clarified, "We ask that they write about what they know and care about. Of course, that means no fiction."

"No fiction?" Nancy asked. "Whyever not?"

"Well, we want the kids to learn how to revise—how to craft their writing until it's focused *and* full of the specifics of real life. So the truth of an experience becomes a yardstick to measure their drafts against. Kids are dying to write fiction, but their stories are more like daydreams on paper. Everything in fiction makes sense to the kid who's writing it, and we're trying to teach them about revising for an audience."

I can only quote Nancy directly one more time. "That's *rubbish*," she pronounced. And she spoke about the stories that children create not as whimsical inventions, but as a kind of fable in which they remake their lives and mingle in the stories they've read or had read to them.

Nancy argued that story writing is, in fact, the most powerful genre for children because it gives them the best opportunities to write fluently and at length. She pointed out that since fiction is about what's *possible*, rather than what's actual, it gives children access to the *hypothetical*: they can begin to see how to improvise on their own experiences. Finally, she concluded that story writing is essential, especially for primary students, because it's the one mode that synthesizes children's experiences, their preoccupations, and their emotions.

I was silent—lost for words. Only after Nancy sprang up to trawl the shoreline for sea glass did a response occur to me. It was a weak one, but it was the truth. I didn't know how to teach fiction: how to invite, respond to, or help children craft make-believe stories. My Boothbay colleagues and I wanted our students' writing to be good, and we hadn't a clue about how to elicit good fiction. So in our writing workshops we continued to steer children toward memoirs and poems—while, as readers, the children continued to live hungrily and happily in the worlds of fiction. We taught them *not* to make believe on paper, even as their minds and hearts yearned, in Ted DeMille's phrase, for "the mother genre."

This was a dissatisfaction that gnawed at my seventh- and eighth-grade writers: they wanted to write what they loved to read. Eventually we found our way together into genre studies of fiction, in which kids and I read compelling short stories written for adolescents and teased out their features. Other middle- and intermediate-level teachers responded similarly to their students' love of stories and desire to write them. But at the primary level, fiction is still, mostly, off the radar in writing workshop—which is the first reason this book is so important.

Ted DeMille has worked hard and smartly to help first and second graders express themselves through stories. *Making Believe on Paper* provides primary-grade educators with the opportunity to learn from an extraordinary classroom teacher about how *and why* to invite and invest in make believe, as Ted demonstrates how he both captures the energy of young writers and balances it with scaffolds and strategies that provide children with the tools to craft their fictions.

As a researcher and critic, Ted studies children's literature that his students like and can learn from, and he identifies the features that make good storybooks work. He goes well beyond the standard prescriptions—e.g., a story has a beginning, middle, and end—to help young writers become aware of and have names for the subtleties of technique that lead to effective writing and illustrations.

Today I teach my seventh and eighth graders in the room adjacent to Ted's writing workshops at the Center for Teaching and Learning. His minilessons about fiction often stop me in my tracks as I'm passing through. I pause to watch, listen, and learn as, drawing on both the mentor texts of published storybooks and his own writing and sketches, Ted demonstrates to his kids such elements of fiction as story language, classic themes and archetypes, story problems and solutions, turns of events, details and dialogue that reveal, inclusion of main characters' reflections, inviting leads, sensory descriptions of setting, and narrative structure—from the introduction of the main character and his or her problem to the rising action, climax, and resolution of the story.

Similarly, Ted taps mentor texts, along with his own demonstrations of techniques of illustration, to teach his students about the important match between writing well and drawing well. They learn about such artistic fundamentals as filling the frame, balance, perspective, background, foreground, horizon line, and the meaning conveyed through details, most significantly in the facial expressions of the characters.

This reliance on mentor books by author-illustrators such as Kevin Henkes and Arnold Lobel leads to the creation of *innovated* texts. This isn't copying; rather, it's a guided observation and assimilation of some of the fundamentals of plot and character development—as Ted puts it, "a long-distance apprenticeship" that's based on "a proven-effective structure incorporating literary devices that are known to work."

Ted's students thrive as apprentices. In Vygotsky's phrase (1978), they lean on folks who are "a head taller" than they are in the creation of their stories and illustrations, and then they go beyond the adult models and bring their own needs, voices, and perspectives to the scaffolds they've been shown.

Significantly, Ted reminds primary-level teachers that "child-rendered fiction may look different from fiction written by an adult, but is just as valid." He walks teachers through his process as a reader of the drafts of a handful of his students' stories, and these close readings and sensitive analyses are among the highlights of the book. Detailed and revealing, they give teachers a new prism for how to look at and respond to young children's fiction.

Finally, Ted's responses in his conferences with his students are models for the profession. He offers gentle, specific guidance as he talks to children, writer-reader to writer-reader. He describes his confusions, makes observations, offers suggestions, and praises. His delight in his students' efforts is palpable. Here is the adult voice we want in every child writer's ear—a voice of warmth and genuine curiosity. When Ted reads a student's story, he can't wait to learn what happens next.

Tellingly, Ted compares the young child's process of writing fiction to "leaving the safety of home to have an adventure." But his students don't travel alone. They're accompanied by Kevin Henkes, Arnold Lobel, Joy Cowley, Dr. Seuss, Mo Willems, and other great authors and illustrators. And they're both followed and led on their journeys by a teacher that Nancy Martin would have adored. Ted DeMille leaves a trail of bread crumbs that any primary teacher can trace into the fantastical forests of make-believe.

NANCIE ATWELL
Center for Teaching and Learning
Edgecomb, Maine

Reference

Vygotsky, L. S. 1978. *Mind in Society: The Development of Higher Psychological Processes*. Cambridge: Harvard University Press.

*I*t would be impossible to mention all the people who have helped me reach the point where I had enough knowledge and confidence to humbly attempt to write a book. Some of you are unforgettable.

First I need to thank Florence Rossman from Wheelock College who in my first graduate school class told me I could write. That changed my life. Florence was an important mentor to me and countless other Wheelock College graduates. I owe her a debt of gratitude that can never be repaid.

Hildred Simons from John Winthrop School for Young Children was my first boss. Her relentless advocacy for newly initiated learners was inspiring and memorable. I think of her every time I speak to a child. She shepherded me through my Wonder years of teaching with tough love and credited me for being like a sponge when it came to learning. Hildred, you were the water.

I would be remiss to leave out my primary song-writing partner and musical mentor, Simon Huntington. For over twenty years Simon and I have worked on our songwriting craft and created songs that are memorable and meaningful to the Bluegrass music community in the Northeast. Along the way I have learned that the writing, revising, editing, and publishing process with children is nearly identical to the work Simon and I do together. I thank him for his commitment and gift of time and friendship.

Many teachers at the Pond Cove School in Cape Elizabeth, Maine were influential to my learning, but Deborah Jordan Pearson and Susan Welch stood out among the crowd. Deborah, one of the finest kindergarten teachers I have ever worked with, taught me the importance of consistency and how to set up an elegant, student-friendly environment. She was a most cooperative colleague, able to hold her end up in any discussion, and never lost her grace when the chips were down. Sue guided me through my first years in public education and in many instances I should have listened to her more carefully. Her wisdom is immense. Of the many gifts Sue bestowed, perhaps the greatest is that she put me on the road that first led to Maine and then to The Center for Teaching and Learning (CTL).

My time at The Center for Teaching and Learning has been more challenging and satisfying than I ever thought possible. I want to thank all my current colleagues: Helene Coffin, Jill Cotta, Glenn Powers, Sally Macleod, and Katie Rittershaus for sharing the path with an abundance of compassion and good humor. I'm glad to have found a teaching home among such wonderful, caring, and professional people.

And of course, deepfelt gratitude goes to Nancie Atwell for starting and sustaining a school where the type of research and curriculum development I do is supported, welcomed, and encouraged. CTL is an oasis in a hard and difficult world. Nancie continues to be an inspiration to me and to so many other professionals in our field. I'm blessed to count her as a mentor and a friend.

I also need to thank Nancie for providing me with opportunities for presenting my work professionally and for putting me in touch with the good folks at Heinemann who have been more than patient with a first-time author. I especially want to thank Patty Adams for guiding me patiently through the rapids of production editing, Lisa Fowler for brilliant photography of me and my students, Alan Huisman and Elizabeth Tripp for expert manuscript editing, Leigh Peake for her encouragement, and Zoe Ryder White for skillful editing help on the first few drafts.

Speaking of Heinemann, my intrepid editor and Walloon Institute boss, Harvey "Smokey" Daniels, was never more than a phone call away as he crisscrossed his way from coast to coast during the years it took me to complete the manuscript. His advice and good judgment about the content and structure of the book always made sense. Without his steady hand, clear vision, and gentle nudging, I never could have completed even a first draft.

Finally, I owe a great and ever growing debt to the hundreds of students that I have had the privilege of teaching in Maine and Massachusetts over the past twenty-six years. Each and every diamond day they have taught me the lessons about life that I need to learn.

$\mathcal{L}$ ong before I could read, I listened to the stories my parents and grandparents told me. Favorite along-side gripping World War II yarns and tales of the Great Depression were my elders' retellings of classic fairy tales and stories of their own devising. Among my first memories, I am sitting on my mother's lap, listening to her gentle voice tell her own versions of *Little Red Riding Hood* and *Jack and the Beanstalk* to pass the time on car rides and picnics and to get me to go to sleep each and every night. When I grew tired of those old favorites, she and my father would tell tales off the top of their heads or (as I later learned) adapt the plots of movies or television shows they'd seen but I hadn't. These were dramatic and exciting—stories of cowboys and Indians, stories about knights and dragons, tales of the American Civil War.

As I got older and my literacy circle widened, I would travel with my mother to the Lower Mills Library in Dorchester, Massachusetts, where I discovered that many of the fairy tales I believed members of my family had made up were written down and illustrated. Next door to these on the shelf were stories with the same plots my parents had cleverly invented. I'll never forget the warm amber light streaming through the high cathedral-like windows of the old brick building. And in a way it was a cathedral—my first temple of good literature.

Among the pile of truck books and easy readers I would choose to take home, there was always at least one fairy tale and at least one fictional story. Being a city boy, I loved the rural, bucolic settings in places long ago and far away, places that looked familiar yet had a hint of the exotic. The rolling hills and deep forests held wonder, mystery, and a touch of fear of the unknown. I was drawn in by the rich character descriptions. I wanted to *be* the children in these stories. There was fascination for me in leaving the safety of home to have an adventure. The stories filled me with confidence that one day I could go out into the world and seek my fortune the way these brave and intrepid characters did. I felt for them and took their problems seriously. I hung on every line of print as they worked against enormous odds and overwhelming obstacles (evil stepparents, giants, and clever stalking animals). I delighted when they emerged victorious through hard work, cleverness, and good fortune. I marveled at their determination to carry on even when their prospects appeared dim.

I especially liked stories in which the characters worked together, forming alliances to defeat a common foe. And at the end, the evil, selfish, or greedy character always got what he or she deserved. These fair and just endings, although sometimes brutal, helped teach me a sense of right and wrong. The character I was rooting for, often a child protagonist around my age, was restored to the ones he loved and was cherished by the community as a hero. This hero or heroine was often embraced by the same adult characters who initially called him foolish and warned him not to take on the quest or fight the giant or were angry that he traded the cow for the magic beans. In the end, those adults who called the young heroine foolish become impressed by the girl's survival instincts and her ability to outsmart the lying father, the evil troll, and the prince who provided unfair choices.

I found I was drawn to stories with similar archetypes. You can argue that these archetypes are buried in much of great adult literature. For all their complexity, at their core most of the classics are stories of right and wrong, pitting good characters against evil characters. Most contain elements of redemption, and most feature main characters triumphing over amazing obstacles against overwhelming odds. I was absorbing these archetypal story structures at an early age, and I have always kept room in my heart for fairy tales. I believe that my initial experiences with fairy tales paved the way for my understanding and enjoyment of all the other types of fiction.

I grew older and read more widely. I was lucky to be born into a family of readers. Everybody read all the time. I remember my dad, his glasses pushed down on his nose, lying on the couch engrossed in his latest World War II book or biography. For her work, my mother was constantly reading patient case studies so she could figure out the mysteries and causes of hospital-acquired infections. For recreation, she read mildly trashy novels (usually on the beach) and lots of magazines. I recall tagging along with her to the hairdresser, watching with fascination as she read *Life* magazine with her head under one of those enormous pastel-colored hairdryers. My older sister, Wendy, was a major influence on my reading. When I was very young she read to me, and as I got older she turned me on to a great number of pop culture magazines, which I devoured. *Rolling Stone* and *Tiger Beat* were the best.

Even at an early age I remember my family talking about books at dinner. We had a little family book club each night at the dinner table. My dad incorporated elements of the stories he was reading into his nightly shares, and I hung on every word. He in turn listened patiently to *my* retellings. In fact, my whole family took great satisfaction in my malapropisms and innocently profane first-consonant substitutions. I was raised Catholic and attended my first High Mass when I was six or seven. I was enthralled by the way Father Lennon sang the liturgy, similar to Gregorian chanting. I was drawn to the ancient and mystical quality of his voice. I wanted to try it out for myself. When I got home from Mass, I ran upstairs to my room and picked up *Green Eggs and Ham* and began to read the gospel according to Seuss aloud. Apparently excitement overtook me and my singing and chanting grew louder and louder until it reached the ears of my family members downstairs. When I paused for breath, I could hear them howling with laughter. It was my first experience unintentionally performing for an attentive and appreciative audience.

I was learning about the power of books—the connection between reading and sharing good stories and interesting factual information, the retelling of a funny or suspenseful passage in a book, or simply reading to gain information about what time Bonanza was on or how the Red Sox had done the day before. It was what the grown-ups did, and I wanted a piece of the action. I learned that books could be central to the enjoyment of and participation in community. As a member of a community of readers, I had the right to read what I wanted to and the responsibility to share what I read with others.

I realize that immersion in good literature and learning the fundamentals of story construction have been central to my enjoyment of life, my success as a teacher, and my ability and desire to write poems, stories, and songs. My love of reading and writing has added depth and complexity to my life experiences. Early and deep encounters with books have helped me better understand people and provided me with touchstones I use when connecting with strangers, acquaintances, friends, and those dear to my heart.

In this book I share strategies I've developed to make the study of fiction a reality in the primary classroom so that our very youngest students have many opportunities to fall in love with the world of fiction not only as readers but also as writers. This book is an invitation to explore—initially with me and later with your primary students—the possibilities and opportunities available in studying and writing fictional stories, including fairy tales. Along the way I'll show you the distinct elements of fiction that my first and second graders have discovered and labeled. I'll talk about the importance of knowing these elements well before writing, outline several activities and the lessons I use to teach them, and discuss the importance of great storytelling and rich literature. We'll look at using author studies and mentor texts to enhance your students' understanding of and ability to write quality fiction.

My hope is that through reading this book, you'll see that writing fiction can be a vital element of and a natural companion to your and your children's reading program. All the color children's writing samples in this book are also shown on the companion website in full color. Please note that the web icon indicates to go to the website, books.heinemann.com/demille. Here is an original fairy tale my student Eoin, a second grader, wrote at the conclusion of our fairy tale study:

For a full-color version of this child's work, please see the website, books.heinemann.com/demille

The Map

by Eoin Anderson

For a full-color version
of this child's work,
please see the website,
books.heinemann.com/demille

"The Map" by Eoin Anderson

Once upon a time there live a cow named Eoin. He lived under an oak tree in a field. His favorite food was sweet grass. There was one thing special about him. He had a map.

Eoin liked to go to new places. He was very nice. If you got near him he would just say moo. Most of all he loved the different animals that lived near him— except one. His name was Devil The Crow.

"The Map" by Eoin Anderson *(continued)*

Devil was evil. He always stole the food from all the other animals. His feathers were pitch black and his claws were as sharp as nails. He always made the other animals mad, but most of all he loved maps. Maps told him where all the food was...and he loved food. He knew Eoin had a map and he wanted it.

One day Eoin saw some good green grass far away, so he went to get it. When he turned around he couldn't see his oak tree, so he got out his map to look at it. Right when he had figured out the way back, Devil came and snapped up the map with his beak and flew away.

Devil flew to the top the highest mountain he could find. Eoin couldn't get up that high, but he remembered looking on his map. He remembered that there were stairs on the back of the mountain.

Eoin went to the mountain and found the stairs. When he got to the top he saw Devil and Devil had the map. Then Eoin said, "Hey, look! A cheeseburger!"

When Devil turned around Eoin took the map and climbed down the mountain. Devil followed close behind.

"The Map" by Eoin Anderson *(continued)*

On his way back down the mountain he saw Devil. Devil said something that surprised Eoin. Devil said, "Can I be your friend?" Eoin saw in Devil's eyes that he really meant it, so Eoin said yes.

When they got back to the oak tree, Eoin gave Devil the biggest plate of cookies he had ever seen. Then Eoin asked Devil, "What is your name?" Devil said, "Devil." Then Eoin said, "From this day on everybody will call you Angel."

There's nothing like getting lost in a charming and exciting story like Eoin's. There's nothing like melting into a well-established, beautifully described setting like the cow's field or being swept away by a classically rendered lead in which the main character is a cow who loves maps. There's nothing like meeting a lovable character you care about and can understand: Eoin the cow, with his obvious love for the animals around him and his affection for sweet grass. Can't you imagine approaching him and waiting for him to "just say moo"? There's nothing like being introduced to an evil and despicable crow like Devil. There's nothing like experiencing the gradual rise of action and anticipating the clash over the map, the small and interesting details of the chase, and the cow's use of brains over brawn as he plays on the crow's gluttony and gullibility to restore his treasured map at the story's climax. Finally, there's the gentle slope down to the story's resolution. Eoin's choice to redeem the evil character in the end not only displays his skill and understanding of the fairy tale genre but also reveals that he is a good and decent person who tries to see the best in all people.

My students often create stories like Eoin's, and yours can, too. Each piece of writing will be as unique as the kid who writes it and will reveal what each writer knows and loves in addition to what she has learned about fairy tales and fiction. You may be wondering if Eoin dictated this story to me, or if his older sister, Maura, wrote it at home and slipped it into our finished-work basket at school. You might ask how did Eoin write it, and how long did it take him to complete, and how much help did he get? Well, that's what this book is all about: showing you every step we may go through as teachers to release stories like Eoin's from kids' imaginations. There's nothing like a good made-up story, and the only place to find it is in the pages of a fiction book, the type you and your students will soon be writing. So let us begin.

Teaching Children to Write Fiction

en years ago I could not have written this book. I was teaching kindergarten near Portland, Maine. I had what I thought was a solid kindergarten writing program sanctioned and supported by my school administration, designed by me and my colleagues after carefully reviewing the latest literature, and respected by parents. Each day after snack time, my five- and six-year-old kindergartners dutifully (and, in many cases, joyfully) took out their homemade journals and began drawing and writing. Sitting cross-legged on the floor, their journals on wooden boards on their laps, or lying on their bellies, their journals on the floor, they would draw colorful rainbows, hearts, self-portraits, pets, families, and playground scenes. They would draw cars, trucks, gymnasts, ballerinas, soccer players, the changing seasons, and occasional superheroes.

Gradually the markers were pushed to the side and a pencil became the tool of choice as each student labeled his picture using approximated or invented spelling. The children did their best to remember the minilesson of the day, in which I had bestowed on them a brief (five- or ten-minute) pearl of wisdom about a particular writing convention. They worked hard to leave a finger-width space between each written word, to use a capital letter at the beginning of a sentence, to put a period or exclamation mark (renamed *stop signs* and *screamers*) at the end of a sentence.

As they worked, I made my rounds with my clipboard, checking each child's progress. Had they retained the skills I had covered in the minilesson? Were they able to use them independently? Were they forming letters from top to bottom and from left to right? Did the writing match the picture? I looked for teachable moments. I stopped and offered support, reminders, redirection, and praise. I made notes on my clipboard to inform my future teaching. When the twenty- to thirty-minute writing block was over, everyone would regroup and two or three students would share their work. Classmates would make positive comments about the drawing and writing shared. The journals were then placed on the shelf until the next day.

My goal was to nudge my kindergartners forward and help them become better writers. But was I really doing that?

In part I was. In his song "Child of the Wind," songwriter Bruce Cockburn says of observation, "[it] depends on what you look at obviously, but even more it depends on the way that you see." I was a commanding teacher of writing conventions. Each year I and the other members of the kindergarten team got high marks from our first-grade colleagues, who told us that our students came to first grade with the ability to form letters, space words, use simple forms of punctuation, and spell most sounds contained in words—all important and essential skills to use when attempting to make sense on paper and provide your audience with an easy reading experience. But that is all I looked at, so that is all I saw.

Then I moved to Edgecomb, Maine, to work as a first- and second-grade teacher at the Center for Teaching and Learning (CTL). Before starting at CTL, the only time I'd heard of the school was on the snow-closing notices on the television. "What do they *do* up there?" I'd wonder out loud. Then I met Nancie Atwell, CTL's founding director, and began my personal journey with the workshop approach to teaching.

CTL has been described as a very unusual yet ordinary school. It is nestled in the rolling hills of midcoast Maine in a sleepy little village called Edgecomb, a river town located on the banks of the Sheepscot across from its more affluent and well-known sister, Wiscasset. CTL was founded in 1990 by Nancie Atwell as a faculty-run lab school where teachers and students could collaborate on growing and sustaining the workshop approach to teaching and learning. For the next eighteen years, that is exactly what has happened.

CTL is by no means a school for rich children. Because of our commitment to a heterogeneous student population, our students' parents represent many walks of life. They include fishermen, carpenters, teachers, boatbuilders, bank tellers, an electrician, a seamstress, and sales clerks, as well as physicians and lawyers. More than half of the children receive some form of tuition adjustment. In addition to tuition, which covers about 65 percent of school costs, CTL is supported by donations from teachers across the country, an annual fund-raising campaign, grants, and revenues from a visiting-intern program and school-sponsored conferences. My mixed first- and second-grade classroom population closely mirrors that of a typical rural Maine elementary school. If you were to come and visit (an opportunity open to you through our intern program), you would find me dealing with typical classroom problems. As in all American schools, there is a range of student abilities, personalities, and learning styles apparent in our classrooms. In our primary classes we have children who have gotten an early start on reading and writing at home and others who come to us as emergent readers and writers. In many cases, drawing is initially more accessible than writing for our students.

Our academic approach, however, is unique. We differentiate instruction for all. At each grade level and for every subject, instruction is organized as a workshop. Class meetings begin with a whole-group minilesson, and each lesson is followed by time for individuals to try out new skills or concepts in the context of authentic activities monitored by the teacher. In the workshops, teachers introduce the standards and conventions of writing, reading, math, history, science, and the arts; children apply these to independent projects; and teachers circulate among their students to confer with and help each child, reinforce what they have taught, and introduce new skills and concepts in context.

In 1998 I found myself at CTL, grateful, excited, and a little scared. This was the kind of teaching I had dreamed of doing, but as always, we must be careful what we wish for. The learning curve was steep, and I quickly came to terms with the fact that I was going to need to go back to school and open myself to the learning process. Once I gave myself that license, doors opened up that I never knew existed. In mid-September I realized that the way I had defined a competent primary writer was rather limited.

At CTL I have learned to teach my students the procedures and craft of writing *good literature*, including letters, poetry, songs, memoir, nonfiction, biography, and, of course, fiction. This still includes conventions—they are staples, and children need to learn them—but doesn't end with conventions.

My Assumptions About Teaching

Before exploring the specifics of what and how I teach, I need to acquaint you with a few assumptions about learning I've made over twenty-five years of teaching.

Primary kids thrive when they are comfortably placed in the apprentice position while a more experienced learner takes on the mentor role. Educational psychologist Lev Vygotsky wrote about the importance of social interaction in learning and pointed out the power of this special relationship. Throughout history, education has been conducted by apprenticing younger, less experienced learners to older, more experienced mentors, to the mutual benefit of both parties. Social interaction and communication occurs while the mentor and the apprentice engage in authentic, purposeful work.

One of Vygotsky's most important theories is the idea of the zone of proximal development, or ZPD. Simply paraphrased, this is the spot on the learning continuum at which the learner needs help from a more skilled person to accomplish a task she cannot do independently but is ready to attempt with support. A teacher's most important job is to recognize these teaching opportunities and take advantage of each teachable moment. After identifying a ZPD moment, the teacher takes steps to provide the learner with the skills, strategies, or information that he needs to continue the task being attempted. The goal is to extend the creativity and self-reliance of learners as they strive for independence, autonomy, and knowledge.

Today, I teach my students to read each learning opportunity, to try to make sense of it, and to consider their options given the knowledge and experience they possess. I invite them into a learning *relationship*. I encourage them to take advantage of the learning opportunities that are available, including asking for help when they need it from me or other adults they trust.

Nancie Atwell has taught me three important sources that a teacher must draw on to teach any academic discipline:

1. *Personal experience of teaching and learning: one's own learning and reading about teaching and learning.* As a teacher, I need to know how to provide information in a vari-

ety of ways that my students can understand. I have to be well versed in teaching methods, and I need to know how to connect with the students and make my knowledge accessible to them. I need to demonstrate my own struggles and joys with learning. I need to be the most experienced reader, writer, and researcher in the class and share my techniques, skills, and strategies with these less experienced—but eager and creative—learners.

2. *A general knowledge of the needs, tastes, and passions of learners of a particular age.* As a teacher of primary school children, I need to know the ways and stages of my particular group. What makes each stage of development unique, and how will this understanding affect my teaching? What particular materials will I need to match the tastes of my students in reading workshop? What kinds of writing materials will they be drawn to and make good use of? What strategies will I use to teach craft, conventions, and procedural information during workshop minilessons? A skilled teacher knows the developmental range and needs of her students.

3. *Specific knowledge of particular students and of each child's intentions and needs as a learner.* Perhaps this is the most important of the three. There is no time better spent than developing relationships with your students. Learning the likes and dislikes of each child can help you put the right book in the right hand at the right time. Finding out what your students collect, what pets they have, their food preferences, what they are good at, and whom they admire can help you suggest compelling books and writing topics. Learning each child's fears, hopes, wishes, and dreams can help you become more sensitive and respond with more understanding in and outside the classroom. (I share the same information about myself with students.)

In this way we are able to develop a classroom community in which each child is known by others. Through letter writing, questionnaires, lunchtime conversations, emails, revising and editing writing, conversations, recess games, phone conversations and porch talks with parents, and occasional eavesdropping, I collect this information throughout the school year and use it to connect with my students. It helps me solve both academic and social problems. The more I know about my children, the easier it is to respond to their academic and social needs. This is not an extra thing to do—it is an *essential* thing to do. Social relationships drive my program. There is no substitute for the serious, ongoing work of nurturing relationships.

I have heard teaching described as an art and good teachers as artists. It is a good metaphor and one I readily accept. But it can be easily misunderstood. As they do with visual art, when people discuss good teaching, they are often looking at an end product: a skillfully delivered lesson, a final copy of a book a child has written, a boy or girl reading aloud fluently, even (gasp) an achievement test. Examining these products in isolation is like looking at a finished piece of art in a gilded frame hung in a museum. But so much work precedes the beautiful finished product.

Two of my favorite artists are Claude Monet and Jackson Pollack. When you view a Monet or a Pollack masterpiece at an art museum, you see the painting finished, complete. The Monet is quietly spectacular: the choice of setting, the quality of light, the softly muted pastel shades, the delicate brushstrokes of a master filled with skilled intention. The arresting dribbles of Pollack are arranged to conjure the feeling of a tiger without ever showing you the figure. The purposeful swirls and drops, wild and fierce, are a visual metaphor for the animal that is the painting's subject. Each of these painters, arguably at different ends of the artistic spectrum, share the intentionality that most often produces works of art. We look at the paintings in museums and are impressed and moved at how the paintings make us think and feel.

I love the finished products my students create, and I relish getting the job done, but I also know that so much goes into the work, everything from a well-conceived lesson to an especially productive interaction with a child. Being a teacher, like being an artist, is on many levels a messy job. A film of Jackson Pollack at work shows us a man covered with paint and constantly moving—conceiving, planning, implementing, and evaluating. He has an idea of what he wants to accomplish but is open to opportunities that arise on the canvas while he is painting.

To Pollack, the outcome and the process seem of equal importance. To me, the same goes double for teaching. The way we teach fiction to primary-grade students has a direct impact on how well they learn it and what sort of outcomes they create. I invite students to become, as Vygotsky might put it, young apprentices to me and to worthy writers of children's literature. As Nancie Atwell taught me, I make a deal with them that we will develop relationships based on mutual respect and hard work. I let them know that they will do real writing, not just exercises or practice, and that I will take their writing seriously. I invite them to build with me and their class-mates a community of writers, all of whom will be focused on get-ting better at communicating through drawing and writing.

Why I Teach My Students to Write Fiction

Fiction has a specific structure. There are fundamentals to learn, skills and strategies to master, and messes to be made on the way to finished products. Before I came to CTL, I looked only at writing conventions, but now I see fiction as an ambitious, magical, and teachable genre for primary students. I can look at and identify the components of fiction and demonstrate them to my students so they can consciously and unconsciously internalize these elements and begin to make the genre their own. You can, too.

My main reason for writing this book is to make a strong case for including fiction in primary school writing programs. We don't teach fiction enough, and I've always wondered why. We are miss-ing a huge opportunity. Teaching children to write fiction makes sense and is important for the following reasons:

1. *Kids love to make up stories.* Is this too obvious to mention? Dreaming up tales and stories is simply something kids do, whether we encourage them or not. Storytelling arises natu-rally in their play, alongside their drawing, and in kid conver-sations in which the real and the made-up very comfortably coexist. There is a rich literature going back decades about the universality, the complexity, the psychology, and the artistic quality of children's spontaneous fictions (Pitcher and Prelinger 1963). Kids want to spin stories; we should let them.

2. *Fiction is the mother genre.* For most of us, our entry to liter-acy as very young children is through fiction: storytelling, fairy tales, folktales, ghost stories, and myths. If you ask

adults to name some of their most powerful and precious childhood memories, many will readily recall getting tucked into bed, cuddling up with their parents, and having a story read to them. For others, it may be sitting and reading alone in the big armchair in the living room, getting lost in *Frog and Toad*, *Stuart Little*, the Hardy Boys, Nancy Drew, or any one of a thousand good books with compelling characters. Most children want to read or be read to, which may account for the popularity of story time in both bookstores and classrooms. In spite of the recent and welcome boom in nonfiction for children, the most beloved literature in the primary years is still fiction. All twenty-seven authors listed on Wikipedia's (January, 2008) "Children's literature" page as making significant contributions to children's literature are fiction writers. Under the heading "Genres of Children's Literature" on the same page, fiction reigns supreme: only fiction authors and series are mentioned. The best-selling children's books of all time are dominated by fiction books such as *The Poky Little Puppy*, by Janette Sebring Lowrey; *The Very Hungry Caterpillar*, by Eric Carle; and the previously mentioned *Green Eggs and Ham*. Of the last fifty Newbery Award winners, all but a handful have been fiction.

3. *Fiction teaches us.* Some of the most influential lessons we learn come from the books we read as children. In all cultures, fiction is a method of passing on important survival information and culturally important themes. This is the way newly initiated members learn the customs and practices of the tribe. It is how young people are taught the respected ways of being and doing. Each ancient culture had ways of passing on this information around campfires or in tribal councils. Fairy tales were introduced orally as cautionary tales to warn children of the dangers around them and to remind them of how society expected them to act.

4. *Fiction brings to light universal and archetypal conflicts and metaphors.* Fiction helps children grapple with normal childhood fears such as injury, abandonment, and powerlessness (Bettelheim 1976) and helps them see how a person might triumph over enormous challenges as characters escape mighty and evil enemies and accomplish

impossible-seeming tasks. Stories often feature characters who gain wisdom through suffering, who are generous and selfless, or who overcome their selfishness and prideful behavior. We are shown the righteousness of humility over greed and the triumph of the youngest, weakest, or most oppressed in the face of overwhelming odds. Fiction and fairy tales value risk taking over sitting still and cleverness over the status quo. These qualities are admirable and attractive to primary students.

5. *Fiction is, arguably, the most challenging, satisfying, and sophisticated of all forms of writing.* It is what first comes to mind when we hear the word *literature*. Above all other genres, we revere the made-up stories in novels and plays that powerfully combine artistry and experience. This is what we consider the highest form of writing. Creating original fiction (writing literature) lets children tap all the power of the ultimate writing experience.

Given that reading fiction is essential to our growth as individuals and as cultures, why isn't *writing it* seen as equally vital? Other genres get far more attention in school writing programs. Elementary students routinely write memoir, language experience stories, and informative and persuasive pieces. Probably the two most popular elementary writing programs today are Ruth Culham's Six Traits and Lucy Calkins' Units of Study. Though very different from each other, both approaches emphasize personal narratives and informational writing over fiction. Indeed, very few state standards encourage fiction writing. Instead, most state tests stress functional and informational writing. And if the state tests don't cover it, in many places it doesn't get taught. Are we are afraid of or uninterested in kids' real stories? Are other genres (science reports, five-paragraph themes) safer, more predictable, or more functional?

As is true for most youngsters, my favorite stories when I was a child were made up. While I enjoyed learning about animals and nature, my heart and mind belonged to make-believe. I spent hours listening to the stories of my parents, grandparents, and older friends. I spent much of my day and every night reading fiction or having fairy tales and storybooks read aloud to me.

I even admit to having a casual relationship with telling the truth. My earnest accounts of my day often included chance encounters with lions, tigers, and bears (who often spoke to me), elephants who scaled the fire escape of my first-grade classroom, and hungry, pitiful dogs who walked into school begging for the parts of my lunch that I didn't want to eat. In all cases I was heroic, kind, brave, and otherwise accommodating to these creatures—unless it was my duty to vanquish them for the good of humanity and in order to save my own bacon.

My mother was quite patient with me and good-natured about these fabrications. In part I believe she enjoyed the entertainment and was fostering my creativity. I also believe she didn't see any harm in the stories or any need to compel me to tell the truth in all situations. Plus she had an equalizer: she would listen and react and even ask extending questions during the tale and then would calmly ask me, "Is this a real story or a Teddy-made-up story?" I would insist each of the stories was true, but my smile and laughter would give me away. It was a game just the two of us would play. It is a treasured memory. When I write about it, my mother appears to me as real as if she were alive today.

The game was so enjoyable that I was always inventing new experiences to top the last. Along the way I incorporated all types of ideas, settings, characters, story problems, action, details, and endings from books, television, popular culture, nonfiction information, personal experience, and school information to make my stories better. Some of the best grist for the mill came from the filmed versions of storybooks I saw on *Romper Room, Captain Kangaroo*, and *Rex Trailer's Boomtown*. Here I first experienced Virginia Lee Burton's *Mike Mulligan and His Steam Shovel*, Robert McCloskey's *Make Way for Ducklings*, Crockett Johnson's *Harold and the Purple Crayon*, and a number of other excellent and inspiring works of fiction. I recall the camera skillfully moving in for a close-up on a character or an action or pulling out to establish a setting, much the way Ken Burns does today in his documentaries on baseball and the Civil War.

At an early age I was well acquainted with the structure of fiction. It was a huge part of my home and family life. But, curiously, it was not recognized at school. I was a product of the Dick and Jane era. I read the controlled vocabulary stories, and while I very much enjoyed Eleanor Campbell and Keith Ward's pastel watercolor depictions of the idyllic early-1960s suburban lifestyle of Dick, Jane, Sally, Mother, Father, Spot, and Puff, I was not inspired by these stories and believe that I learned more about reading from the fiction I encountered at home. I don't recall any of my primary teachers reading storybooks aloud to me. Except for the yearly play we performed, fiction and fiction study didn't make a strong impression until third or fourth grade, when we were allowed to go to the library and take out books to read independently at home.

School would have been much more interesting and exciting for me had it included more storybooks and fairy tales. I was ripe for reading experiences that mirrored what I was reading, watching, making up, telling my mother, and acting out in real life. It took a while for schools to catch on to the power and quality of children's fiction. Fortunately, fiction stories are now part of even the most skill-driven basal reader programs, and many schools have adopted literature-based reading programs in the primary grades.

Programs have changed to reflect more closely young children's love of fiction. Children's hearts and minds still belong to make-believe. You see it in their play and in what they choose to read, listen to, and talk about. You also see it in what they write about unprompted during their free time. Recently Jacob presented me with the story on the following pages in my honor, which he had written at home.

I was thrilled and delighted by this charming story. I was honored to be the main character. I was also curious about how the story came to be. I knew Jacob read from the Dr. Seuss box at school and had some experience with rhyming stories. He was a playful and energetic student. The next time I saw his mother waiting on the porch when school was dismissed, we discussed the book. I told her how much I had enjoyed it, and she said with a smile, "Jacob does this all the time. Every night he sits down and makes books."

That triggered something in my memory. As far back as 1981 and my first classroom teaching experiences, every time young writers (even those as young as four) were given the opportunity, they made books like Jacob's. Given the training and the time, students grabbed sheets of paper, stapled them together, and wrote stories. Most of the time their stories blended their own life experience with the fiction they were reading, just as Jacob's story does.

Writing fiction allows children to combine what they know, what they love, and what they want to do. We bombard children with

For a full-color version
of this child's work,
please see the website,
books.heinemann.com/demille

"Ted in a Sled" by Jacob

great (and sometimes not-so-great) storybooks, audio- and video-
tapes, television programming, and oral storytelling. Along the way
we provide ample opportunities for them to learn the structure and
elements of fiction. We expose them to so much fiction, good and
bad, that they become adept consumers. They begin to evaluate
and discriminate on their own.

"Ted in a Sled" by Jacob *(continued)*

TED WENT OVER
A SKI GUMP IS
he GONOOW BE DAED

I DONT THINK 2O
BUT he LANTED
IN A SNOW
BED

"Ted in a Sled" by Jacob *(continued)*

But while we do an excellent job exposing children to fiction in school, we hardly ever ask them to write their own stories. Why is that? You'd think with all the time and energy we put into providing excellent stories to motivate children to read, we could see that we are ignoring an excellent model for teaching them how to write. In addition, explicit teaching of the structure and elements of fiction would go a long way toward helping children comprehend, predict, infer, evaluate, and enjoy what they are reading.

Helping children write fiction is what this book is all about. If we help children understand how to write fiction early on, they will become better readers and writers. They will understand how stories work and be able to express themselves through stories inspired by the great stories that have come before.

My Teddy-made-up stories are lost in the fog of years past. The memory of the relationship they helped me build with my mother endures. There are so many wonderful and unique stories waiting to be appreciated. Children are capable of documenting the stories that lie dormant in their imaginations. We simply need to show them the structures and elements that already exist in the grand tradition of storytelling and story writing. We need to show them what good authors do to craft exceptional fiction. We have to set aside classroom time during which young writers can craft, illustrate, revise, edit, and publish stories. We need to appreciate who they are and what they are capable of as writers and individuals. Like good parents, we need to be reflective and open-minded about content while gently reminding them of the difference between fact and fiction. We need to appreciate that child-rendered fiction may look different from fiction written by an adult but is just as valid.

In the pages that follow I will encourage you to consider Jacob's (and other students') inclination to craft interesting and sincere fictional stories—to make believe on paper. Let's elevate the writing of fiction, give fiction the time and attention it deserves in the curriculum, and see what stories primary students can share with us. We need only show them the way.

2 CHAPTER

Paving the Way with Reading Aloud, Storytelling, and Art Instruction

*I*n order for children to write stories like my pal Eoin, the creative pumps need to be primed with rich book, language, and art experiences. By including these three important strands in your language arts curriculum, you can build kids' excitement about and understanding of fiction.

Reading Aloud

In a 1985 report by the Commission on Reading titled *Becoming a Nation of Readers*, one finding stands out above all others: "The single most important activity for building the knowledge required for eventual success in reading is reading aloud to children." Not phonics, but reading aloud. Orville Prescott said in his book of poetry *A Father Reads to His Children*, "Few children learn to love books by themselves. Someone has to lure them to the written word. Someone has to show them the way" (1965). And Jim Trelease (2006), the author of the perennial best-seller *The Read-Aloud Handbook*, reminds us on his website that "we read to children for all the same reasons we talk with children: to reassure, to entertain, to bond, to inform or explain, to arouse curiosity, to inspire. But in reading aloud, we also condition the child's brain to associate reading with pleasure, create background knowledge, build vocabulary, [and] provide a reading role model."

All this is the pleasurable job of parents and classroom teachers everywhere. The benefits are countless:

1. *Reading aloud demonstrates that reading is a shared experience of joy for the reader and the listener.* When reading
   aloud, a more experienced reader researches, chooses (after
   rejecting several other possibilities), introduces, reads
   aloud, and then discusses a favorite book with less experienced readers he cares about in order to educate and
   delight them. By consciously including children in this
   important bonding activity, we initiate the youngest literacy
   learners into the reading club. Above all, we read to kids
   for the irreplaceable delight and engagement it provides.

2. *Reading aloud helps children develop listening skills.* When
   a story is read aloud, time often seems to stop. Children
   are hushed and completely focused, as if a spell has been
   cast. Inside that spell, there is room for a few questions
   and comments by the reader and listeners, but too much
   time spent away from the text is frowned on. This is in
   stark contrast to watching television, an experience in
   which (even when it is not punctuated by repeated channel
   switching, as it so often is) interruption and broken concentration are built in by the inclusion of commercials.
   When children are engaged as participants in a read-aloud,
   real listening is happening. They hear the words being read
   and put the ideas together with the pictures shown on each
   page. They are totally engaged and active in the process. I
   know, because they make insightful comments about the
   text during and after reading. They tell me when I have
   skipped a page or missed a particular part of the story.
   When the book is exceptional, the whole class enters into
   what one of Nancie Atwell's classes labeled "the reading
   zone."

3. *Reading aloud helps children develop language skills.*
   Reading aloud to children regularly helps them master
   vocabulary and language concepts. Children begin to store
   information about sentences, paragraphs, context, gram-
   mar, syntax, and word meanings. When they are ready,
   they use these ideas in their own reading and writing.

4. *Reading aloud helps children understand story structures
   and storybook language.* Reading fairy tales helps children

understand the elements of fiction used in most fairy tales, important baseline information for understanding and making inferences about the genre. Reading a variety of other fictional texts acquaints learners with common features such as rhyming, question-and-answer formats, the idea of redemption, and the bad-events-that-turn-to-good-events structure. Understanding these features is essential to being able to write fairy tales and fiction. We'll look at some of these elements in later chapters.

5. *Reading aloud demonstrates the behavior of a good reader.* Reading aloud shows the entire class that teachers are readers who solve problems. Though we typically read books that we know and love well, our performance is rarely perfect, and kids can learn much from us when we have to work hard, right in front of them. Indeed, some experts say we teach kids more skills when we read books aloud cold, without much practice, thus revealing the process we go through to figure out unknown words as they come up. While in most cases when reading aloud, you should practice and prepare, occasionally minilessons that feature cold reads can be informative and instructive. Young readers see how we overcome difficulties to make sense of the text. Reading aloud gives us the opportunity to demonstrate and discuss all the relevant reading strategies:

   - Look at pictures for clues.
   - Follow left-to-right directionality.
   - Match each word with its articulated sound.
   - Use initial and final letter clues.
   - Seek out rhyming or repetitive patterns.
   - Say sounds slowly.
   - Speed up or slow down according to the difficulty of a passage.
   - Find the tricky word elsewhere in the text.
   - Guess and ask: Does it look right? Does it sound right? Does it make sense?
   - Skip the word, read to the end of the sentence, then go back to the beginning of the sentence and try again.
   - Look for the big word in the little word.
   - Read dialogue and attend to meaningful punctuation.
   - Ask for help.

In my primary classroom, I read aloud as many as four or five storybooks per day and at least two chapters of a novel during quiet time. In addition, I *book walk* as many as five or six books each day, introducing my students to new and different books or old favorites of mine that they have not yet experienced. I also try to connect specific children to specific books based on their interests in a particular subject or genre. (Nancie Atwell calls these *reading territories*.) In our school's first trimester, each child, after my demonstration, makes a map of each of his or her reading territories. I keep these in mind when I'm browsing in the bookstore or at a yard sale for books to add to our classroom collection.

When I read aloud, I follow these guidelines:

■ *Whenever possible, read books that you love.* Reading a book you are less than enamored of shows. Kids can tell, and whatever you were hoping to gain because of the content of the book will be lost. Try to find a vehicle that you can get behind. Life is too short to read books you don't love when you have a choice. That is a good lesson to demonstrate and teach to young readers.

■ *Practice reading the book ahead of time.* Reading aloud is a developed skill. It is a public performance, one that requires preparation. Read through the book prior to reading it aloud and match the text to your reading skills and personal style. If you know what's coming, you'll know what parts of the text to emphasize and when to read the words with a loud or soft voice or give them a funny or ironic twist. You can also decide whether you want to use different voices for the various characters' dialogue and so on.

■ *Before reading, introduce the book to the class.* Frame the event with a short and interesting preview. This could be a brief summary of the setting, characters, or problem; a connection to another storybook you've already read; or a tidbit about the author. These introductions separate the read-aloud from what you were doing before and gently alert everyone to settle in and focus.

■ *Choose parts of the book to highlight.* Identify a few key points you may want to stop and discuss while you are reading. Be careful not to stop too often, and make sure what you are mentioning warrants the disruption.

Sometimes it is safer to read the whole book straight through uninterrupted and then stop for discussions during a second reading. With primary-age students it is a good idea to close the book (while keeping your place) when you go off text. If you keep the book open, some younger students may think that your discussion topic is part of the story. Features of a book you might discuss prior to or during a read-aloud include the following:

- *The various elements of fiction.*
- *The quality and type of illustrations.* Illustrations can be anything from cartoons to high-quality reproductions of museum artwork. Identify the type of art and the reasons the author and illustrator might have made this choice. Did the artist use watercolor paints, oil paints, crayons, collage? How did that affect the story?
- *Information about the author or book.* I spend hours haunting publishers' and authors' websites, learning about authors' lives. I particularly like to learn how an author got an idea for a book or what events in his life inspired certain plot twists or characters. It is amazing how much fiction is based on real life. I love sharing this information with my students, and they love learning this insider gossip: it helps forge a connection between them and the authors. It also shows young writers that they can get ideas the same way their favorite authors do—by writing about real events and by focusing on what they know and love.

Sometimes something wonderful comes up in a book that I overlooked in my preview. An especially choice lead, an effective description of a setting, and a concisely drawn character are all things worth stopping for and mentioning. Just be careful to keep track of time and pick and choose what to stop and talk about.

- *Leave time to discuss the story afterward.* Anything you didn't mention during the reading you can cover after you have finished the book. I always observe a few moments of silence after completing a read-aloud. Often a student will be the first one to speak about a particular feature of the book she noticed or loved. That starts a round of discussion that is often hard to stop. I then return to my preview information and close that loop as well. I frequently use the discussion to tease out elements of the author's craft or reading strategies that I'll cover in an upcoming reading minilesson. When we are focusing on fiction or fairy tales, I introduce activities that teach the elements of fiction.

Storytelling

One way all primary school students can communicate important information about themselves is to tell a story. While not every student is able to convey information in writing, storytelling is something almost all children do well naturally. That's why we should provide a structured time during our regular school day for children to tell stories.

A number of years ago I was lucky enough to visit a classroom in the Boston public school system, where Mary Ellen Giacobbe and Martha Horn were consulting with talented classroom teachers and aides. Storytelling was a big part of what I saw in action that day.

One boy told a brief story about something true that had happened to him, an everyday event. The entire audience could relate to his story about visiting the local barbershop for a fancy haircut. We all listened with respect and rapt attention. The boy made every attempt to use words to shape his story carefully, because he knew we were all listening. When he wandered from the point or stopped, not knowing what to say next, his classroom teacher stepped in to check her understanding of the story so far or ask a clarifying question. This helped the child be more specific so we could all know and understand what he was telling us about.

At the conclusion of the story, audience members had an opportunity to raise their hands and share what they understood about the boy's story and what they wondered about. The boy responded to their comments with additional clarifying information.

In the first chapter of their wonderful book *Talking, Drawing, Writing*, Horn and Giacobbe (2007) make four strong points about why it is important for children to tell stories:

■ Inviting children to talk about themselves and what they know honors them for who they are.

■ By telling stories orally, members of the class immediately get to know one another.

■ Telling stories acknowledges talk as having an essential place at the core of writing.

■ Telling stories orally allows children to learn about the elements of craft before they ever put them on paper.

After seeing this kind of storytelling in action, I came back to CTL and carved out a time for storytelling in my writing program. It was immediately effective. While the majority of the work that Horn and Giacobbi did was in kindergarten, I find the same dynamic in my first- and second-grade classes. The storytelling has a direct and positive impact on my students' writing. It builds a bridge they use to cross from talk to text.

Horn and Giacobbe (2007) list and explain five elements of writing that children begin to understand as they "craft stories with words":

■ *Writers are specific with their information.* After telling a story, my students remember and record many more details in their memoirs than they did before, even if the memoir isn't based on a story they have told out loud. Telling and hearing more specific stories each day helps them remember to add more interesting and compelling details because it is through specifics that listeners and readers come to know and understand.

■ *Order and organization are important.* My students quickly take to the structure of storytelling and are able to create a story line that makes sense. When a child doesn't, I tell back the story in a logical order that sometimes differs from the student's. I notice that my students' work is much more logical than ever before. Having told the story once, they have a deeper understanding when they record their words on paper.

■ *Audience matters.* Writing takes concentration. Maintaining a quiet environment allows students to concentrate on drawing and writing. Before I added storytelling to my classroom activities, I had been troubled by spontaneous chatting between two or three children at one or another of the worktables. Now these table conversations hardly ever happen. The information has already been shared and the problems solved during the storytelling and discussions. In addition, my students now have little fear of public speaking. They are eager to participate and relish the opportunity to share their stories in front of the group. They also get immediate feedback from audience members' body language, facial expressions, questions, and comments about their understanding. The storytellers learn that they have to include certain key elements if they want the audience to understand their stories. They are able to transfer this process to the memoirs they are writing.

■ *Talking can help you think your way into a story.*
Storytelling is an opportunity for writers to organize and order the story prior to writing it. It gives them a chance to get feedback from other writers in a structured setting. This work off the page helps them develop a clearer sense of how to proceed on paper.

■ *Composing involves revising.* As Horn and Giacobbe write, the stories the students start out telling end up very different, yet "the two images seem to lead naturally into one another" (17). The children in my class catch on and need very few adjustments after they have told two or three stories. The daily practice of telling and listening to stories helps them develop their composing skills. That in and of itself is a type of oral revision. (17)

We begin storytelling in September, very soon after the year begins. My approach sticks close to the techniques I observed in the classroom I visited in Boston, with minor adaptations. We begin by gathering in the meeting area in a *bunch of grapes* formation. I use this metaphor because grapes coexist on the vine very close together with minimal bruising. I like this style of sitting because children have the opportunity to sit closer to the book or leader and see and hear more clearly. They also learn how to sit close without difficulty. We observe the following rules: touch nothing but the rug, make sure you can see, and if you need to make an adjustment, do so quietly and without disrupting anyone or anything. It takes some time, but the class generally masters this formation in the first few weeks of school.

Once we are seated, we sing the storytelling song to the tune of "The Farmer in the Dell." (I shamelessly copied this from the Boston classroom.) The words are a simple but effective introduction:

> It's storytelling time,
> It's storytelling time.
> Hi-ho the dairy-o,
> It's storytelling time.

I choose storytellers at random. I have small wicker basket. On the rim of the basket I clasp clothespins, one for every student, labeled with his or her name. Each day we unclasp the number of clothespins equal to the number of stories we have time for (usually two), and these students get a chance to tell a story. I then place their clothespins in the basket along with the clothespins of students who have already told stories. When all the clothespins are in the basket, we put them back on the rim of the basket and start afresh.

One of the storytellers takes the chair I usually sit in, and the listeners follow our regular meeting rules for paying attention. This is not hard for them. Storytelling is a naturally captivating activity for both the storyteller and the listeners. Often the day's most rapt attention is paid during storytelling time.

At the start of the year, the stories children tell are about true personal experiences. Topics should be about common interesting events that have occurred. I demonstrate prior to the students having a turn. Here's an example:

> Today I'm going to tell you a story about something that happened to me when I was in kindergarten. It is a story about me and my mother.
>
> When I was in kindergarten, I lived in the city of Boston. I lived in a small part of the city called Dorchester. I lived close enough to my school that I didn't have to take a bus or drive in a carpool like you do. I walked to school. I really liked walking to school. In the first part of the school year, September to January, I got to walk to school with my sister and our across-the-street neighbors Steven and Keith. But in January, my kindergarten class met in the afternoon, and there were no kindergarten kids from my neighborhood. I was the only one. So I was going to have to walk to school alone. I wasn't

upset or afraid. I felt like a big kid getting to walk to school by myself.

What I didn't know was that my mother was really nervous and scared that something would happen to me when I walked to school alone, but she also knew how much it meant to me to be independent and on my own. She made a deal with me that she would walk with me the first week, but then after that week I would be on my own.

The first week passed without a problem. I was very excited on the first day that I would finally walk to school on my own like a big boy. I kissed my mother at the door. Bundled up in my flannel snow clothes and carrying my snack box, I headed out the door alone and walked all the way to school by myself. I was proud and independent and on my own.

Years later I found out that my mother couldn't bear the thought of me out there by myself. She was so afraid for my safety that when I went out the front door, she left out the back. She had planned a route that took her through backyards and side streets so she could watch me and make sure I got to school safely. She knew how much it meant to me to be on my own and she allowed me to walk by myself, but she loved me so much she made sure she was nearby in case something happened.

This story works well for a number of reasons. It is short but interesting to the kids. Anytime I reveal something about my life, particularly from my childhood, I create a stronger bond with my class. They get to know me better. Hearing this one, they can imagine me as a child struggling for my own autonomy and independence; they can say, "Hey, he was like me." They relate my experience with my mother with their own. Possibilities for their own stories begin to emerge. They can tell a mother story. Whole genres of storytelling have grown out of the stories that children tell, personal injury being a far-and-away favorite.

Oral storytelling quite naturally invites kids to use the distinct elements of fiction that we will want them to begin using more intentionally in their writing. I talk about these elements in much more detail later in the book. For example, look at the underlying structure of my story:

- ■ *Lead.* I begin with a short preview of what the story is going to be about and at what point in my life it happened.
- ■ *Introduction of setting.* I give a simple introduction of where I lived and where the story takes place.

- *Identification of the main characters.* I am the main character in this story, along with my mother. The storyteller always gets to be the star of the stories, which makes sense developmentally with egocentric first and second graders.
- *Introduction of the problem.* In this story, the problem is my walking to school alone and my mother and I having different feelings on the way it should be handled.
- *Rising action.* My mother and I strike a deal and I begin to walk to school alone and establish my independence.
- *Resolution.* I let the audience in on my mother's subterfuge—what she did to make sure I was both safe and autonomous.
- *Ending.* I conclude by confirming my mother's positive intentions and clever strategy.

Telling stories about true events paves the way most directly for memoir writing, but these fundamental building blocks of literature are eminently transferable to fiction, so it's an easy crossover. We recall how we have been telling true stories and the basic template and structure we've been using. We use these previous experiences to guide us into the new genre.

After a child tells a story, she draws a picture about the most important moment of the story in her sketchbook. Here is the picture I drew of my story to demonstrate:

My mom watched me walk to school with out me knowing. She wanted me to be safe. She didn't tell me she did it until years later. She hid behind fences and trees.

For a full-color version of this work, please see the website, books.heinemann.com/demille

My picture of me walking to school

With this picture in mind, we can begin to discuss the important connection between pictures and words.

Art

After storytelling has been introduced and children become comfortable with the routine, it makes sense to record some of these shared ideas on paper. Connecting the spoken word to pictorial documentation paves the way for writing.

All children can tell stories when they come to school, and most can draw. Many first graders are most comfortable expressing their ideas on paper through drawing. Drawings continue to augment and support the work of young writers through second grade and into the upper primary grades. In my classroom, I want to be sure kids maximize what they can communicate with drawing and art.

Some children are veteran users of pencils, crayons, and markers from their early years at home, in preschool, and in kindergarten. They come to school with small-motor control well established and have a natural sense of some of the fundamentals of figure drawing, perspective, and composition. They may have an innate or early developed sense of which colors complement each other and how to use lines and shape to render an effective drawing.

I want to open the world of drawing to all my students. I don't subscribe to the theory that drawing is a skill that some people are born with, and the rest of us are out of luck. Everyone can learn and use basic drawing fundamentals to communicate better with pictures. I also don't believe that there is one way to draw anything, and I tell this to my students. But if some children in first and second grade are still struggling to draw stick figures, I help them out by showing them how to draw simple people and animals using common geometric shapes. I also introduce the entire class to some artistic fundamentals that give each person more choices when composing a picture.

I have developed a series of lessons over the years, lessons that I am constantly updating and revising as I learn more about my own artistic process through my own art experiences, books I've read, and artists whom I talk with regularly.

The first lesson I do is designed to help students get used to creating the basic shapes and lines they'll use when they draw people and animals:

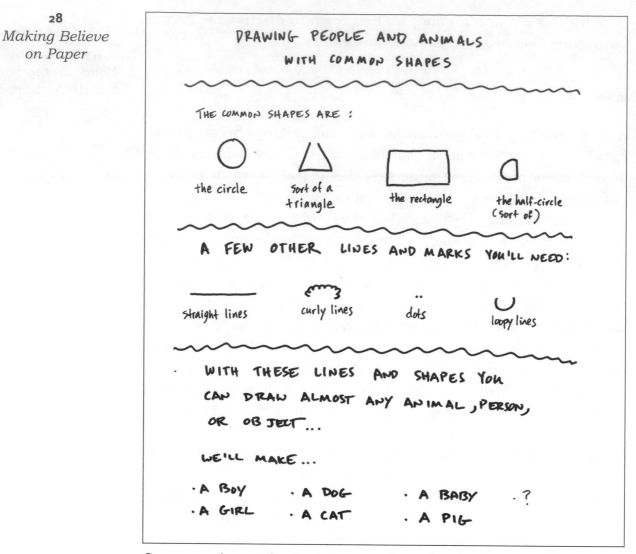

Common shapes for drawing people and animals

I introduce the shapes and lines at a group meeting and demonstrate drawing the lines on large chart paper mounted on a large wooden easel. Each child has a sketchbook with 8½-by-11-inch paper. The students draw each shape and line as I do. I keep an eye on their individual progress and make gentle comments and adjustments as necessary. We practice just drawing the lines and shapes to get a feel for each one and to establish control of the pencil while making each shape and line. It doesn't take very long, since most primary students are very familiar with these common shapes.

When we all seem comfortable, we move on. I reveal what human figures and animals we will draw. I focus on a few common figures that I can draw well and that children need to know how to draw to communicate pictorially. I start by drawing two human figures, a boy and a girl. I tend to start all my drawings from the top. It is a comfortable point of reference for me, and I also use it when I'm introducing letter formation, so I encourage the class to start at the head and move to the feet.

The head is a circle or oval shape. The body is a triangular shape that emerges from the neck region. (The sharp point of the triangle is hidden behind the head.) The legs are also modified rectangles that meet in the middle to form pants. Next I add two rectangular arms that attach to each side of the body. The shoulder line will be longer than the armpit line, unless the arm is raised. I finish the outline of the body with half circles for the hands

THE BOY

1. Draw a circle for the head
2. Draw a triangle like body
3. Draw rectangle like legs
4. Add half circle feet
5. Go back up to the body and add rectangle like arms
6. Add half circle hands
7. Finish up the face with loopy hair, dot eyes, and a loopy smile ... half circle ears, too.

straight hair works too!

A boy

and feet. Next I add details: dots for the two eyes, a curved line for the mouth, and half circles for the two ears. For hair I use curly lines (for curly hair), straight lines (for "spaghetti hair"), or short, bristly lines (for a flattop). I then add any details to the clothing such as pictures, numbers, or words on the shirt and stripes or checks on the pants. I often incorporate a style of clothing or fashion accessory that one of the class members is wearing that day. Finally, I add color using twistable crayons, which have become a staple in my classroom. They offer the same color choices as colored pencils but cover more area faster. They rarely break and last forever, the two main advantages over regular crayons.

As I am drawing, the children are watching. I encourage comments and questions. I ask them what they notice about my drawing and what they remember about how I did it. I remind them that the lines and shapes that I used are all lines and shapes we've used and worked with before.

The next figure, a girl, uses the same basic shapes to form the body but lengthens the triangular shape to form a dress. At this point I often ask for suggestions about how I can make my figure look more realistic. The children offer details regarding hair length, dress color, jewelry, and other accessories they think will augment my drawing. Their own creative juices start flowing, and they are ready to begin their own drawings.

Invariably someone will mention that not all girls wear dresses all the time. I demonstrate how to draw a girl in pants using some of the same techniques I used to draw the boy but incorporating the other strategies the class gave me to make my figure look more feminine. Here's what that looks like:

A girl

A curly-haired girl in pants

After this demonstration, the artists are chomping at the bit to draw some of these figures themselves. We head to the worktables after a few reminders:

- Draw your figures in pencil first. If you make any mistakes, pencil lines are much easier to correct than crayon.

- Don't rush your shapes. You are in control of the pencil. You should work as slowly as you need to in order to stay in control of your lines. Too slow can be a problem as well. Find your own comfortable speed.

- Your drawing doesn't need to look just like mine. You may have other ways that you draw your figures that are a bit different. It is perfectly all right to use those strategies.

- Let me know if you need any help, and I'll come over and take a look at your work and talk about it with you.

The next part of the workshop looks very similar to an art class, but also like a typical writing workshop. Children go to their worktables, open their sketchbooks, get the materials they need from the storage shelves, and begin purposeful work. My first job as the most experienced artist and writer in the group has been to provide a craft minilesson designed to help them communicate more effectively on paper. They are now working with the concept I shared. My next job is to walk the room, determine what they have learned, and offer helpful comments as they are working. I help with subtle line adjustments, sizing suggestions for proportions, and comments about originality and details, and I respond to specific questions the artists have about anything we covered in the lesson. I reteach, remind, and redirect if necessary. I know I've been successful if the drawings the class renders have progressed from stick figures and if the children feel better about their work.

Subsequent lessons build around the figure drawings. People need companions, so we draw common pets, including the cat and the dog:

Farm animals come up pretty often, so we add the pig:

We also add other family members, including parents and babies:

Each figure uses the same or similar geometric shapes and common lines, dots, squiggles, and swirls. All are familiar to the children, and all lessons are introduced and implemented using a minilesson and guided practice. At the conclusion of the mini-lessons, students have mastered several figures. Each of these drawings is safely and securely recorded in their sketchbooks. They have a reference for drawing figures as they create stories. The lines and the formats they've learned from the lessons can be reused to draw any number of additional animal figures they may need to augment the stories they are writing.

As one child figures out an effective way to draw a particular figure, he shares that figure with the class. Here are first grader Carissa's early-in-the-year drawings of a boy and a girl based on the minilessons:

Carissa's boy and girl

You can see how she used some of the strategies I shared but also added features of her own, including necks, smiles, shoulders, a more fashionable and flattering dress on the girl, and longer, more realistic feet on both the figures. Her arms are more animated as well. Her figures include the geometric shapes but also reveal what she has learned from her own experiences with drawing.

This is also evident in second grader Teddy's rendering of a dog and a cat:

For a full-color version of this child's work, please see the website, books.heinemann.com/demille

Teddy's drawings of a cat and dog

He used some of the geometric shapes, including circles and ovals, but has simply and elegantly created unique animals, improving on my model. Teddy's animals have real personality and a real sense of place. He has placed the cat on the green, comfy couch and the dog by the food and water bowls.

Here is Teagan's pencil sketch of a pig from early in her second-grade year:

For a full-color version of this child's work, please see the website, books.heinemann.com/demille

Teagan's pig

There is a real perspective in this drawing, and Teagan has also provided a real sense of setting. This could be the beginning of a fiction story.

Children are also free to blend their own personally developed art techniques with the strategies I'm sharing. In addition to their own art strategies, they also draw, as they write, about what they know and love. Michael was happy to share his free-choice sumo wrestler technique with the class:

Michael's sumo wrestler

For a full-color version of this child's work, please see the website, books.heinemann.com/demille

As the year rolls on, children begin to request specific animals and objects they would like to add to their personal drawing repertoires. We try to figure out the shapes, lines, and dots of these items together.

At the top of the next page are four vehicles Charlotte drew during one such session.

Over time every student becomes better at communicating through picture making. This goes a long way toward creating a community of artists, which in turn leads to creating a community of writers.

Once we as a group can draw figures confidently, we move to some other important art fundamentals that help children create more detailed and interesting pictures. Here are some of the mini-lessons I do each year:

Charlotte's vehicle drawings

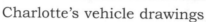

- *Picture frames.* I've noticed that children are better able to create pictures within a boundary. I demonstrate framing each time I do a drawing, and I encourage them to draw a frame for the picture they are trying to make and to work within that frame. This is especially effective when children are drawing pictures to go with print in a booklet or sketchbook. The size of the canvas defines what can be included in the picture and will inform the artist's choices. It also helps when revising pieces of writing in case a student wants to use her original drawings for a final copy.

- *Vocabulary.* I teach a basic artist's vocabulary (including *top, bottom, left, right, background, foreground,* and *horizon line*) so we'll all be on the same page when we talk about art. As I am demonstrating, I use these terms. I also use them when discussing a drawing with a student. I introduce these terms in a minilesson and present the students with a reminder sheet similar to this one:

PARTS OF A PICTURE

. If you can, frame your picture before you start drawing

. Learn the "parts" of your picture...

TOP

BACKGROUND   Right side

HORIZON LINE

FORE GROUND

Bottom

· There is a flower in the foreground.
. There is a car on the horizon line.
. The sun is in the background on the right side.
. A cloud is drifting from the left side over a tree.

Artist's reminder sheet

- *Shapes and lines in nature.* Children have a tendency to draw flat, straight lines when representing nature, which is not always accurate. We spend a good bit of time observing the rolling hills and curving pathways of our Maine environment and reproducing the same shapes in our art. We take into consideration what setting we are trying to represent and get information about what that setting looks like. This research informs the way we proceed with our drawings. This initial discussion about setting sets the stage for fiction writing later on.

- *Perspective and balance.* I demonstrate how objects that appear in the foreground of a picture appear larger than those in the background. I discuss and demonstrate balance. I draw a balanced picture and an unbalanced picture and ask the class which picture makes more sense and looks better. The students say that in the unbalanced picture there are too many things squished together on one side. In the balanced picture the objects are more evenly placed, and that looks better. Often the objects on the outside edges of a picture can be used to direct the audience's attention toward the action in the center of the frame.

- *Filling the frame and using color.* I am a big proponent of filling the entire frame and completing detailed illustrations with vibrant color. I demonstrate these techniques to the children and encourage them to follow through with carefully done, detailed, colorful drawings. To enable them to do this, we keep our picture frames reasonably sized and use twistable crayons that cover space quickly.

How to draw a balanced picture

As the year progresses and as it seems useful and necessary, I introduce other drawing concepts, such as using elements in the landscape to indicate mood (sun to indicate a hopeful story part, rain to indicate sadness) and facial features to reveal character.

———◆———

Reading aloud, storytelling, and art instruction prepare children to write quality fictional stories. Each activity contributes to building deep overall understanding of story elements. Enjoying literature read aloud and developing the ability to talk about literature and understand its ingredients are essential to writing fiction. A personal understanding of how a story is told and regular practice with telling stories to an audience in a safe, friendly, yet challenging environment help kids develop the skills necessary to write fiction. Knowing how to draw detailed figures, animals, and landscapes can inspire and augment fiction writing. By looking at their own drawings, children can often generate ideas to represent in print far more effectively than when they start writing off the top of their heads. Illustrations are essential for the writing of quality fiction books.

And writing books is where we are headed next. The next two chapters focus on helping children emulate fine authors and create original fiction by following in the footsteps of Kevin Henkes and Arnold Lobel.

3 CHAPTER

Choosing and Using Mentor Texts

$\mathcal{M}$ ost creative journeys start with some sort of outside inspiration. My own songwriting was triggered by listening to Bob Dylan, James Taylor, Joni Mitchell, Taj Mahal, Guy Clark, and Townes Van Zant. When I heard their wonderful, specific, transcendent songs, a voice in my head said, *I want to do that*. My first songs were enthusiastic and spirited imitations of what I considered good songwriting. Imitating the masters is universal in all art and is often the first stage in any creative process.

I've destroyed the tapes of those early songs of mine; however, they were not only vital to my future development but also a right and reasonable place to start. In a sense, I began a long-distance apprenticeship with those writers. I studied their craft. I read everything I could about them in *Rolling Stone* magazine. I went to their concerts and watched them on television. I set up my own virtual classroom and was as wide open as I could be to how they did what they did. I learned the fundamentals of songwriting. What words and vowels sing well, how to count syllables so the lyrics go with the melodies, what minor chords trigger an emotional response, when to use metaphor, when too much metaphor is bad, and other skills and strategies that informed my craft.

As I continued my creative process, my own voice began to emerge based on what I knew, what I had experienced in life, and what and whom I loved. I kept the craft, but my work became less derivative of my teachers and more reflective of me. I became a decent songwriter—but I wouldn't have without the entire experience, in particular those derivative beginnings.

I have turned this apprenticeship process into a learning strategy and used it countless times to learn new skills—how to write a book, how to be a better teacher, how to be a more accomplished public speaker, and how to belt sand a front porch.

I also try to reproduce this experience in my classroom. I set up a series of apprenticeships throughout the year and invite my students to sign on. As the oldest and most experienced writer in the class, it is my responsibility to teach my students what I know about writing to help them develop their own skills. I also know all too well that I don't know everything. I need to show my students how other accomplished children's book authors, the equivalents of Dylan and Mitchell, do what they do. We need to enjoy, appreciate, discuss, understand, and emulate the books of the masters, paying special attention to how they pattern their fiction. We need to read about them and learn about their approach and their fundamentals. We need to try their moves on for size in the way that younger kids play dress-up and act out what they want to be when they grow up. In my classroom, we call these kinds of mentored stories *innovations*. By paying attention to what choices talented authors make, we open up a world of opportunity for beginning writers. What begins as imitation or impersonation soon moves beyond that.

This approach to inspiring kids' writing can be combined with an author study or incorporated into a short fiction-writing unit designed to help children identify story patterns, understand and appreciate author voice, and create story innovations independently. The stories I choose are deliberately short (students can complete an innovation in a few sittings) and well within the grasp of most first and second graders, as they should be. If students are to understand and work with the story in a meaningful way, they need to be able to read it independently. Good mentor texts for primary-grade students are elegantly simple and contain interesting language. They are great three-minute rock 'n' roll or blues songs rather than beautiful and lengthy symphonies or string quartets.

I look for several characteristics when I identify a storybook as a mentor text from which my kids can launch their own writing:

- *Length.* The story should be long enough to have some breadth and depth but not so long that an innovation on it will take weeks. Stories between eight and sixteen pages long are best at this stage of development. Longer doesn't mean better. Some of the best stories I've ever read are sixteen pages long.

- *A clear and memorable pattern.* The pattern of the story has to be clear enough for children to remember. Mentor texts should be *holiday reads*, easy enough that children can study the text as a tool for writing, not just use it to build their reading skills. The book should delight and engage students, *compel* them to work with it.

- *Distinctive qualities of a unique author.* In music, we are often drawn to a particular performer because of the distinctive musical and lyrical qualities she brings to the process and final product. I choose teaching texts for those unique qualities that set authors and illustrators apart and make the work individual and special. I want students to look closely at what's effective in a particular writer's or illustrator's work and try the same strategies on for size.

- *Inviting language.* Children's books are similar to poetry or song lyrics. There are only a few words, which have to be chosen carefully, since each word has tremendous impact on the overall story. Some books just sing out—the words roll easily off the tongue and integrate with the illustrations brilliantly. These types of books make outstanding mentor texts because they introduce the children to the writerly craft of cutting to the bone, being economical and discriminating when choosing words.

- *Simple but detailed illustrations.* The illustrations should be simple enough for the students to replicate when they write their own versions. The pictures should augment the meaning of the words. It is useful if the illustrator has used some special visual features such as close-ups, long shots, talk balloons, and other devices that convey extra meaning.

- *A universal theme or classic archetype.* People against nature, redemption, movement from harmony to chaos and back again, a quest, a mother's undying love, being lost and then found—all these classic story archetypes make excellent mentor texts. These are proto-stories passed down from generation to generation, stories we humans respond to time and time again if they are told with sincerity and skill.

Once I find an appropriate mentor text, I follow the same workshop pattern of minilessons, demonstrations, and explications to make the story accessible to my students. There are five basic steps:

1. *Reading the story aloud.* I begin with a large-group read-aloud. I sometimes repeat the read-aloud as a review before we begin looking at the story for meaning and author strategies.

2. *Discussing the story.* During this ten- to twenty-minute session, I ask what the students understand, remember, and notice about the book. I point them in the direction of author strategies and idiosyncrasies I feel are important. This is an important lesson in which we together label what is unique and worth borrowing from a particular author. We define what makes the book memorable, the writer and illustrator special. To borrow a term from Nancie Atwell, we *unpack* the story.

3. *Scaffolding the story.* After we have an idea of what the author did and what we want to emulate, I help the class write a story in the voice of the author, with the important distinction that they must change the characters and the details to reflect their own interests. I want the kids to integrate real experiences into the template the author used. Working together, we rewrite the story as a large group. I demonstrate how to adapt the story using the information we have generated together.

4. *Guided writing.* Each member of the class is now ready to write his own story using our group story as a model. I check each student's progress and walk the room, helping with text and illustrations. Each student creates a final draft in the voice of the author in two or three days.

5. *Following through.* Finally, we revise our texts and illustrations, editing for punctuation, spelling, capitalization, letter

size, and word spacing. We hand our work over to a volunteer typist. If the cranky old computer system cooperates, we can turn our stories around in a day or two.

Now that you know what to look for in a mentor text and how the process works, I'll model this approach using Kevin Henkes' *A Good Day* (2007). (Chapter 4 follows two kids as they do this on their own using the same story.)

Henkes is a skilled and talented writer and illustrator. Here's what he says about himself on the HarperCollins website:

> I remember drawing at a very early age. I loved it. And my parents and teachers told me I was good at it—that made me love it all the more. . . . I also loved books, and the ones I was lucky enough to own were reread, looked at over and over, and regarded with great respect. To me "great respect" meant that I took them everywhere, and the ones I still own prove it. They're brimming with all the telltale signs of true love: dog-eared pages, fingerprints on my favorite illustrations, my name and address inscribed on both front and back covers in inch-high crayon lettering, and the faint smell of stale peanut butter on the bindings. I wondered about authors and illustrators back then—what did they look like? where did they live? did they have families? how old were they?—but I never imagined that one day I would be one myself. (n.d.)

His books are favorites of my first and second graders. He has a deep and visceral understanding of the thoughts and feelings of young children. His very human characters (often anthropomorphic) express their fears, hopes, wishes, and dreams, supported by the strong and steady love of parents and other benevolent adults.

In *A Good Day* Henkes uses a simple and flexible structure to tell a story about "discovery, love, luck, persistence, and a different point of view that changes a bad day to a good day" (Henkes 2008). The story unfolds in three acts. In the first act, each of four baby animals (a bird, a dog, a fox, and a squirrel, introduced in that order) has a problem (Little Yellow Bird loses his favorite feather, for example). The second act takes care of all of the animals' problems, reversing the order in which they were introduced (Little Yellow Bird decides he doesn't need that feather anyway and flies "higher than ever before"). In the final act, a little girl finds the missing feather in her garden and, taking this discovery as a sign of good luck, runs in to her mama, shouting, "This is a good day!" The illustrations are vibrant and simple, resembling old-fashioned woodcuts. Small amounts of print make it an ideal read for kindergartners and a breeze for first and second graders.

I start by reading *A Good Day* aloud to the class the first thing one morning. The students listen with rapt attention. Afterward I ask them what they noticed and understood about the story. They mention (or I point out) the following:

- The are four animals.
- Bad things happen first.
- Good things happen later.
- The little girl finds a feather.
- All the animals are in the final picture.
- The order in which the animals appear is reversed in the second half.

It is clear from these responses that the group understands the main idea and the important details of the story. I'm encouraged, but I want to make sure they truly understand the meaning. I praise them for getting the big idea of the book and tell them, "This story starts off badly for all the animals, but then toward the middle of the book, good things do start to happen for them. The bird's, dog's, squirrel's, and fox's luck changes. This is called a *turn of events*; in this story, things go from bad to good. Another important part of this book is the end, where the little girl finds the lost bird feather and shows it to her mom, saying that it's a good day. That is kind of a surprise at the end."

I end the lesson by summarizing the story and recording the information on a chart. Here's the summary and story sequence:

A Good Day, by Kevin Henkes
A turn-of-events story with a surprise

SUMMARY: Four young animals have bad things happen, but then the day gets better, and in the end it becomes a good day for them and a friend.

Part 1—Bad things happen to the bird, the dog, the fox, and the squirrel.

Part 2—The animals' luck changes! Good things happen to them, in reverse, or backward, order.

Part 3—Then there's more! A little girl finds the bird's feather and tells her mom it's a good day as all the animals look on.

Later in the day we come back to the story with a new focus. I introduce the writing lesson this way: "Today we are going to get a chance to write in the style of Kevin Henkes. I'd like you to try to write and illustrate a story using the idea and pattern of his book *A Good Day*. Here's what I'm thinking: I'd like you to use four animals that you know and love; choose animals that aren't in Kevin's book. Invent problems for these animals like Kevin did for the animals in his story, and then make each of their days get better. In the end, choose a gift that one of the animals can give to a boy or girl in your story that will make it a good day for him or her, just like Little Yellow Bird did for the little girl, even without knowing it! To help you write this story, I've put together a planning page and a chart that might help you solve some of the story problems."

Then I display the following information on a large piece of chart paper:

Writing Plan for A Good Day, *by Kevin Henkes*

A turn-of-events story with a surprise

WHAT TO DO: Write and illustrate a story in the voice of Kevin Henkes using four young animals that you know and love. Invent bad things that happen to them, but then make the day get better, and in the end choose a gift that one of the animals gives to the boy or girl in your story that makes it a good day for him or her.

Part 1—Start off with the words "It was a bad day. . . ." Invent bad things that can happen to the four animals you choose.

Part 2—Start with the words "But then . . ." Make the animals' luck change! Choose four good things that happen to them, in backward order.

Part 3—Write, "But there's more. . . ." Have your child character find the treasure the animal left and run to tell someone.

I go over the chart with them, paying particular attention to the phrases indicating time and its progression: "It was a bad day. . . ." "But then . . ." "But there's more. . . ." I explain that these are structural phrases that keep the action moving. We discuss whether or not it's necessary to mention every little thing the animals have done or whether the action keeps moving because Henkes tells only about the events most important to the story.

We also talk about the fact that the first animal introduced in the story needs to lose something a child will consider a treasure and what kind of animal that might be. We brainstorm a variety of possibilities, including a snake, various types of birds, and some imaginary animals like dragons and unicorns.

Then we discuss other types of animals they can choose to fill out their cast of characters. The class agrees we should keep Henkes' idea of using baby animals. As a scaffold, I provide the following table, which they can use as they choose the animals for their story and define the bad and good things that will happen to each of them:

Animals	Bad Thing	Good Thing
Gift animal		

Introducing the table, I say, "Write the names of the animals you choose one by one, top to bottom, in the 'Animal' column. Then fill in the bad thing that happens to each animal in the 'Bad Thing' column, and finish the table by filling in the event that solves the problem and makes it a good day in the 'Good Thing' column. Let's try it together."

This is the story-planning table we complete as a class:

A Good Day by Kevin Henkes
Table for Choosing Animal Characters and Story Problem

animals	bad thing	good thing
shark Gift? tooth	lost his favorite tooth	forgot about the tooth and swam deeper and faster than ever before
dog	couldn't find his food bowl	found bowl on porch filled with food
horse	lost her shoe	farmer helped her put a new shoe on
lizard	lost his tail	grew back a better tail

I can see the wheels of their imaginations turning as they think about what animals and problems they will use to create their own stories. I continue, "When you have completed your table, you can make a booklet.* You'll want to use at least six folded pages." Since this is a new use of the booklet, I demonstrate again how to make one, reminding the writers to orient the booklet with the spine (stapled side) *to the left*. Next I demonstrate how to add illustration boxes to the first few pages. I also add page numbers, circled, in the middle bottom of each page.

Keeping the table we have generated as a group alongside me, I

---

*I got the idea for the booklet (a device I also use when my students are writing fairy tales, nonfiction, and memoirs) when I noticed that whenever they had free time during the school day, many children would ask if they could staple pages together and make a book. Now, at the start of the year when we are learning all the necessary procedures that help writing

I model making my own booklet. Using a pencil, I create a cover with the title *A Good Day*, skipping a cover illustration for the moment:

Cover of class' *A Good Day*

Next I begin the first page of text. "Let's look back at the book to see how many words the author used and what ideas he showed on each page. What words did the author use on the very first page to introduce the first part of the book?"

"It was a bad day," the children say in unison.

"Should I use those words, too?" I ask.

workshop function smoothly, I teach students how to use the stapler safely and show them our paper shelf. They learn how to stack their sheets of paper on top of one another, even up the edges, fold the sheaf of papers in half, and then staple them together (once near the top, once near the bottom, and once in the middle of the folded side). I keep several previously made booklets on hand for those who find making them difficult.

"Yes!"

I write those words at the top of the page, demonstrating conventional letter sizing, capitalization, and word spacing.

Next I say, "Kevin used a little drawing of stripes on this page. I want to add a little more meaning. What drawing could I use to show that it was a bad day? For example, what kind of weather could I draw?"

Colin offers, "A hurricane!"

"That would be a really bad day. I don't think I want my day to be quite that bad. What would be a little less bad than a hurricane?"

Sophia says, "How about just a rainstorm?"

"That will work," I say, and I begin to sketch clouds and raindrops with my pencil (I don't add any color yet). "A rainstorm matches the sadness that the characters might feel in the first section of the book, when things aren't going well. Illustrators often use weather to help tell about the feelings of the characters. In this book I want to do that, too." (I'm introducing an important craft concept here: illustrations can help establish the mood of the characters. I'll return to this concept frequently when reading aloud and making books.)

Now I am ready for page 2. I ask the group, "What was the first animal we chose to include in our story?"

"The shark," they reply.

"And what happened to the shark?" I ask.

"He lost his tooth!"

"Let me check my table to make sure we got the animal and the words in the right order."

I look at the table and run my finger over to the first box and find the information about the shark and his tooth. "Yes, it was the shark. Now that you've told me and I've made sure, I'm ready to write the words and draw the picture."

At the bottom of the page, I add the words (inspired by Henkes) "Little shark lost his favorite tooth . . ." Then I work on an illustration to match the print. I begin my sketch of the underwater scene. I move with care but not at a snail's pace. I try, as always, to do a reasonably careful job in the limited time I have. If I make a mistake, I erase and redraw. I start with the ground line, plants, sand, and shell, establishing the setting for the character. Next I draw the outline of the finned shark. Then I add the mouth, teeth, and gills.

Inside pages of the class book

The final touch is the tooth falling to the ocean floor. In about two
or three minutes, my pencil sketch is complete. Here's what my
page 2 looks like:

Inside pages of the class book *(continued)*

So far, I've demonstrated how to construct a booklet, how to put the book title on the cover, how to refer to the table to recall the drawing and text information, how to add text inspired by Henkes' language, and how to complete a pencil-sketch illustration. I don't want to overdemonstrate. Checking the faces of my writers and illustrators for understanding or confusion, I decide to demonstrate one more page to make sure the pattern of referring to the table to get ideas for the text is set, show how to add text, and reinforce my expectations for carefully drawn illustrations in a reasonable amount of time.

"My table tells me I should do the dog page next. This dog couldn't find his food bowl. I used to feed my dog on the back porch. I'm going to use that idea in our book. Remember, in a fiction book, it is OK to use information from your life and to use animals that you know about and love—and are able to draw well. I'm pretty good at drawing certain kinds of dogs."

I start with the text: "Little dog couldn't find his food bowl." I then work on my illustration of the perplexed dog at the bottom of the stairs, wondering where his bowl is. I include a frowny face and a question mark above his head to indicate confusion. Will the kids notice? I'm just about to talk about what I've done when Ella raises her hand.

"Why did you put a question mark over the dog's head?"

I turn her question over to the group. "Does anyone have an idea why I did that?"

A few children raise hands. I call on Colin.

"It means he doesn't know what's going on . . . ah . . . where his bowl is, I mean."

"That's right, Colin. Where have you seen this done before?"

"In Charlie Brown comics."

As I continue to draw, I explain that as a part of my own craft, I do borrow from cartoons. "Adding talk balloons and punctuation helps your audience understand how your character is feeling. My dog character is confused, so I put a question mark above his head. As Colin said, I got this idea from comic strips that I've read. You are welcome to try out adding punctuation and talk balloons in your own stories."

I sense it is time to turn the kids loose to complete their own tables and begin writing and drawing their own books. They understand both the structure of the book Henkes has written and what they need to do to write their own versions of *A Good Day*. Wanting to set expectations for today's writing workshop, I ask, "Do you think you are ready to make your own table using your own characters and think of your own story problems?"

"Yes!" is the resounding response.

"Great," I reply. "Today, let's do three things. First, fill out your table by listing your animals, their problems, and how these problems get solved. Second, make or get a booklet. Third, work on the first part of the book up until the point when the animals' luck changes from bad to good. If you need help, I'm here to give you a

Inside pages of the class book *(continued)*

hand. And don't forget that you have our writing plan and the table you'll make to help you as well."

I send each of them off with a copy of the writing plan, a blank organizer table, and a booklet. At each of our four big wooden work-tables, I have already placed a toolbox filled with pencils, pens, and markers. The writers find their seats and get to work. I grab my status-of-the-class sheet and begin my rounds, checking in with each child to discuss the characters chosen and the problems and solutions to be used and to make sure the first character is one that can leave an appropriate gift behind. A recurring point I make is to keep the story simple and Henkes-esque.

My Henkes-inspired story in its entirety concludes this chapter. The next chapter documents the innovations of two of my students.

Complete book of Henkes-inspired *A Good Day*

Complete book of Henkes-inspired *A Good Day (continued)*

56

Little green lizard lost his tail.

⑤

But then...

⑥

Complete book of Henkes-inspired *A Good Day (continued)*

Little
Green lizard grew a longer and more beautiful tail.

⑦

Little brown horse got a new shoe from a helpful black smith.

⑧

Little dog found his food bowl on the porch and it was filled all the way to the top.

⑨

Little gray shark forgot about his tooth and swam deeper and faster than he ever had before. But there's more...

⑩

Complete book of Henkes-inspired *A Good Day (continued)*

A little boy found the shark tooth and ran shouting, "Daddy, it's a good day!"

⑪

CHAPTER 4

Sophia and Avery Write Like Kevin Henkes

et's follow a couple of my kids as they use mentor author Kevin Henkes as a model for their own fiction writing.

Sophia Has a Go

Sophia is a second grader with a passion for horses, drawing, and friendship. She is a hard worker and can sustain her focus for long periods. She is self-directed and internally motivated. She has a good sense of humor and knows how to ask questions to get the information she needs to solve problems.

When she sets to work on her Henkes innovation, she has plenty of ideas, as reflected in her initial planning chart on the next page.

The progression of Sophia's work from table to draft to final copy is fascinating. Her table indicates a solid understanding of the original text. She has chosen animals wisely based on what she knows, loves, and has the ability to draw. Her table is specific enough to give her a clear and usable outline but flexible enough to allow her to augment the meaning with her illustrations. Ready to go, Sophia makes the transition from planning (or as Nancie Atwell calls it, *writing off the page*) to her twelve-page booklet.

Sophia works on her first draft over the course of two days. Working alongside three other students, Sophia is focused and diligent. She consults her table when she needs to and works through a few problems, the biggest being that she has used a permanent

**A Good Day by Kevin Henkes
Table for Choosing Animal Characters
and Story Problem**

animals	bad thing	good thing
Gift? horse horse show	horse loste his horse Shoe	horse's owner gave him a new, Snow
Cat	little cat lost his Ball of yarn	little Cat found catnip toy
hermit Crab	hermit crad grew out of his shell	Little hermit crad moved to a bigger Shell
Monkey	lost is banana	little Mon-key found a Big Big banana

Sophia's story-planning table

marker on her page 3 illustration, and it has bled through to the other side of the page. To make a repair, we cut a plain white sheet of paper to size to cover the bleed-through. We use a glue stick to adhere it to the affected paper and, bingo, a brand-new blank canvas.

Right before Sophia illustrates her last page (a girl in a garden finding a horseshoe), she comes to me with a question. "How would you draw a garden?"

I ask her to bring me her booklet and a blank piece of paper. "How do you want the garden to look?"

"I want to show the vegetables and the place where the girl is digging."

On the blank piece of paper I draw a horizon line. Below the line I draw an angled rectangle that shows dimension. "This would be one way to draw a garden. If I add vegetables to the rectangle and then color it in brown around the plants, it might work."

"Thanks, Ted." She takes the sketch and her booklet and heads back to work.

During the course of the week, I note on my status-of-the-class sheets that Sophia has written five pages on the first full day of work and an additional five pages the next day. She asks if she can take her book home that night and finish her draft. I tell her that's fine, and she brings her completed first draft back the next day. See below and the following pages.

As is customary in our classroom, Sophia takes her completed draft to a worktable during writing time and completes an editing checklist. (I designed this form to help primary-grade students with the daunting tasks of proofreading and editing. Prior to meeting with me, the writers use the form as a guide when they look over their texts and illustrations for any errors in content or meaning. They also have an opportunity to correct any capitalization, punctuation, letter-sizing, and word-spacing errors they notice in the text.)

For a full-color version of this child's work, please see the website, books.heinemann.com/demille

Sophia's *A Good Day* complete draft

it Was a bad day...

①

Little horse lost
his horse Show.

②

Sophia's *A Good Day* complete draft *(continued)*

Kitten loste his
yarn ball.

③

Sophia's *A Good Day* complete draft *(continued)*

Little hermitcrab moved into a bigger, most taller shell.

(8)

Little kiten fawnd a cat nipe toy

(9)

Sophia's *A Good Day* complete draft *(continued)*

But thars more ...

Thanks!

Your welcome

Little horse's onner gave him a new betr show than evr befor.

(10)

(11)

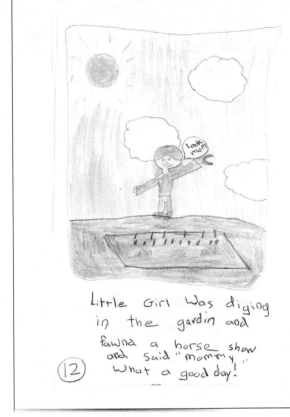

Sophia's *A Good Day* complete draft *(continued)*

While composing a story, it is often hard for young writers to focus on more than writing strong content and completing detailed and careful illustrations—and that is plenty. Therefore, when the draft booklet is finished, it is a good idea for the writer to step back and look for simple errors she might have missed when getting the story down. The editing checklist reminds Sophia to look for errors in the conventions of writing and to identify three words she thinks she might have spelled incorrectly. On the next page is the editing checklist Sophia brings to our conference.

Ted DeMille
January 2008

Name __Sophia__   Date __1/20/08__

Editing Checklist

Title of Piece of Writing __A good day__
I checked for:

☑ punctuation at the end of each sentence

☑ a capital letter to start the first word of each sentence

☑ a capital letter to begin names of people or places, days of the week or months of the year

☑ spaces between each word, or a place holding · or —

I found 3 words I'm not sure I spelled right.

1. ___fownd___
2. ___byger___
3. ___gardin___

Ted's Comments

Sophia's editing checklist

Preparing for a Conference with Sophia

I look Sophia's story over the night before our scheduled conference and prepare some notes on the writing and illustrating choices she has made. This is not a particularly onerous or time-consuming process.

I make notes primarily to document each writer's progress throughout the year. The notes focus on what the writer has done to *make meaning*—the writing and illustration skills he is developing to tell the story and engage the audience. I consult these notes periodically to monitor student progress and share that progress with parents. I also use the notes to prepare for individual writing conferences with students. I want to be ready with questions, comments, and suggestions for revision. At each conference I take a few minutes with the student to work on editing punctuation, spelling, letter formation, letter sizing, and capitalization. I find opportunities for individual teaching moments with writers in each of these realms, and I also look carefully for classwide trends. If I see many children, for example, not utilizing silent *e* in spelling patterns, I know it may be time for an additional writing minilesson on that topic. You'll see loads of these moments in the following pages as I work with Sophia.

Here is Sophia's story with my sticky notes attached:

For a full-color version of this child's work, please see the website.

- followed Henkes model
- used correction tape to fix the Sun
- represented each character in the story well
- composed each picture with multiple layers

A Good Day

by Sophia Stafford

My prep notes on Sophia's cover

Sophia has followed Henkes' lead for the cover of her draft. She includes each character in her title illustration. She includes the story title and a byline and orients the book conventionally, with the spine to the left. She has revised the illustration featuring the hermit crab on her own using correction tape. She has also edited her title to include capital letters, something she hasn't done before. Each of her illustrations shows good command of composition strategies. She has used multiple layers and sound perspective techniques. She has framed each of her pictures as well. Her words are conventionally spaced and her letters are suitably sized.

My prep notes for Sophia's conference *(continued)*

On her first two pages of text, Sophia demonstrates sound understanding of Henkes' story language. She uses short sentences and description similar to the original. In her balanced illustration, Sophia shows sound composition strategies: multiple, rolling layers; animated, moving clouds (one disappearing off the page); lightning strikes; the barn in the background appearing smaller than the horse; and an attempt at a multidimensional fence surrounding the barn. She uses a question mark to indicate the horse's confusion about the missing shoe. The horse's head hangs down and he wears a frown. Her words are conventionally spaced and the letters are well sized. There are a few opportunities for editing: the initial lowercase *i* in the first sentence on page 1 and the word *show* (*shoe*) in the sentence on page 2.

- great drawing of reclining cat (could teach the group)
- reminder not to use the permanent marker for roof
- continues to experiment with perspective (rug)
- weather (lightning)

Edit spelling "loste" — lost

Kitten loste his yarn ball.

My prep notes for Sophia's conference *(continued)*

Page 3 is highlighted by a skillful drawing of a reclined cat on an oval rug, wondering where his ball of yarn has gone. Outside the house, lightning strikes out of the clouds. But the interior of the house lacks details. I make a note to ask Sophia about this during our conference: *What would the inside of the house look like?* Why ask this question? Because this illustration creates a slight disequilibrium for me as a reader. It disrupts my reverie. More detail in this illustration could provide more meaning, so I want to know what Sophia thinks about it, what direction she might go to make this picture clearer. (It's also useful to remember that this is a first draft; nothing is set in stone.) Editing on this page will focus on the misspelling of *lost*; Sophia has added a silent *e*. So far she has used conventional punctuation on pages 1, 2, and 3.

My prep notes for Sophia's conference *(continued)*

On pages 4 and 5, Sophia introduces her hermit crab and monkey characters, both well drawn and delightfully animated. The hermit crab features hilariously bugged-out eyes looking at his too-small shell. I wonder how she was able to cartoon a hermit crab so well. (When I mention this to her parents, they tell me Sophia and her younger brother, Jacob, have raised and cared for a long sequence of hermit crabs. Encouraging children to write about what they know and love never fails to provide information that allows me to get a clearer picture of who they are, helps me build a better relationship with them, and allows me to meet their individual academic and social needs.) The monkey's outstretched arms on page 5 indicate confusion concerning his lost banana.

Both illustrations are well composed. Both feature a large yellow sun. Even though Sophia completed an editing checklist for the book, there is a problem with the sentence on page 4. This becomes my second revision question: *Does the sentence on page 4 make sense to you?* However, I suspect that when she reads the sentence aloud at the conference, the missing preposition will pop out without my bringing it up. I make a note to remind Sophia how important it is to read a draft aloud once it is finished. Editing possibilities include correcting the spelling of *hrmit* (*hermit*) and *bnana* (*banana*).

The first section of Sophia's draft is a success. I'm totally engaged and looking forward to part 2.

My prep notes for Sophia's conference *(continued)*

On page 6 she uses the same transition words that Henkes and I have used. Her illustration on page 7 of the small monkey with the gigantic banana has me laughing out loud.

The monkey's arms are raised in triumphant joy; he voices the sound "Ymm" in the talk balloon. A bright sun shines overhead and three diagonal clouds float in the blue sky. The spelling of four words on this page needs correction: *fawnd* (*found*), *biger* (*bigger*), *taster* (*tastier*), and *bnana* (*banana*).

My prep notes for Sophia's conference *(continued)*

On pages 8 and 9, Sophia continues to resolve the problems of each of her characters in creative and engaging ways. On page 8, she illustrates a beautiful and colorful shell in which her hermit crab character can take up residence. She writes, "Little hermit crab moved into a bigger, more taller shell." While the shell is taller, I wonder whether the most significant aspect of this shell isn't its bright color. I make a note to ask a third revision question: *What do you think is the most important feature of the shell?* As a reader I am first and foremost drawn to the color, but Sophia may have had a particular reason for focusing on the height. If so, I want to know that. On page 8, I mark the crowded text. "Hermit crab" is run together like a compound word. On page 9, the leaping cat is skillfully animated, yet the house still remains unfurnished. The spelling needing correction on this page includes *kiten* (*kitten*), *fawnd* (*found*, a second time), and *nipe* (*nip*). Page 9 remains unpunctuated as well.

But thars more ...

- borrowed my drawing idea for back end of horse and dialogue
- What did that shoe allow the horse to do? (TENSE)

EDIT:
spell   onner
       betre
       show (meaning)
       evr
       befor

Little horse's onner gave him a new betr show than evr befor.

My prep notes for Sophia's conference *(continued)*

For page 10, Sophia borrows my drawing of the half horse and includes a similar dialogue pattern. She writes, "Little horse's owner gave him a new better shoe than ever before." I wonder what the horse will be able to do with that new shoe. I know Sophia to be an accomplished equestrian. We have talked at length about horse shows in which she has taken part, and I wonder if this isn't a good opportunity for her to bring in some of the specific activities that take place at those events. Thus my fourth revision question: *What could the horse do better than ever before with that new shoe?* Five new spelling words appear on page 10: *onner* (*owner*), *betr* (*better*), *show* (*shoe*, second time), *evr* (*ever*), and *befor* (*before*). Next door, on page 11, Sophia winds her story down using the Henkes transition into the final part of the story. Another spelling word

My prep notes for Sophia's conference *(continued)*

shows up here: *thars* (*there's*).

On the final page of text, Sophia ends her story with a little girl with brown hair (like hers) finding a horseshoe in the garden, which Sophia drew with help from the sketch she commissioned from me. The high horizon line comfortably centers the garden in a blanket of green grass. The girl stands at the top of the hill, raising the horseshoe high in the air. Her talk balloon holds the words, "Look, Mom," echoing the text below. Three clouds float through the air overhead. It is a satisfying ending to a wonderful story. Editing possibilities include punctuating the dialogue with quotation marks and changing the capital *G* in *Girl* to a lowercase *g*. Spelling words are *diging* (*digging*), *gardin* (*garden*), *fawnd* (*found*, third time), and *show* (*shoe*, third time).

Getting ready to confer with Sophia, I look at my notes and pare down what I will deal with. My most immediate job is to respond as Sophia's first audience. I need to tell her what I think is especially good about how she has written and illustrated the book. I want to reveal my opinions as an experienced writer and reader about what she has done that really works. A second job is to ask Sophia specific questions about what confuses me or stands in the way of my understanding the text. I'll limit the questions to four or five. Some will help her clarify her intentions as a writer and illustrator. Some may lead her to make specific changes; some won't. A third job is to help Sophia identify parts of her work that need editing. I want to help her make her work easy for her audience to read; I also need to make sure she is gradually learning how to use the necessary conventions of print that I regularly teach as part of my writing and reading program. Each time I confer with students, we spend a few minutes looking at and fixing up spelling, punctuation, capitalization, word-spacing, and letter-sizing miscues.

As I said before, my goal for the revision conference is not to discuss *everything* on the list of what I've noticed from carefully analyzing Sophia's book. Most of that information will simply be archived so that I can see her progress from piece to piece. I need to decide what makes the most sense to discuss at this conference. First I list the reasons her story works so well:

- She includes thoughtful and well-composed illustrations.
- She uses the Henkes' story language well.
- She writes and draws about animals she knows and loves.
- She uses dialogue and thought balloons to add meaning.
- Her choices of characters, story problems, and solutions are engaging.

Then I list the four questions I have:

- On page 3, what would the inside of the house look like?
- Does the sentence on page 4 make sense to you?

- What do you think is the most important feature of the shell?
- What could the horse do better than ever before with that new shoe?

Finally, I make some notes for the editing part of our conference:

- We'll take a capitalization walk to see whether she can identify the few places (*i* on the first page, *m* in *monkey* on page 5) where she needs to capitalize the first letter of the first word in a sentence.

- I'll zero in on three spelling words: *fownd* (*found*), *show* (*shoe*), and *biger* (*bigger*). Sophia has listed *fownd* on her editing checklist and has misspelled it three times in the text of the story. *Shoe* is also misspelled three times. Sophia has also listed *biger* on her checklist and it will give me an opportunity to talk about doubling consonants when adding *ing*.

Conferring with Sophia

My plan is set; I'm prepared. Sophia and I meet the next morning. We have her first draft and her editing checklist handy. I begin by asking her to read her story aloud to me. She holds the book and turns the pages while I follow along. When she gets to page 4, she reads, "Little hermit crab grow out . . . grew out his . . . huh? Grew out *of* his shell! Oops, can I add that?" I nod, and she adds the word *of* in the right spot. By reading that particular part of the story aloud, she has heard the miscue and revised it on her own.

I listen carefully as she reads the rest of her book. I express concern at the sadness of her characters in the first part of the story and laugh at and enjoy the way the characters solve their problems in the second half.

When she has finished reading, I say, "Sophia, I really think your book works well. You did so much to create an exciting story. Your illustrations are well put together. You used a lot of the layering strategies we've been talking about in class, and your characters have so much expression—I can really tell what they are thinking and feeling. You chose animals that you know, love, and know how to draw well. You did a great job using Kevin's story language, and you changed it to match the characters you used in your book. The dialogue balloons and cartoon punctuation really add to the meaning of your story, and I love the characters, problems, and solutions you invented. They all worked so well. Are there some things about your story I can help you with?"

Sophia says, "One thing I already fixed that didn't make sense when I read it."

"I noticed how you did that. Did it help when you read that sentence out loud?"

"Yes."

"Sophia, I've started to do that with the book I'm writing at home. Reading it out loud helps me check whether it makes sense. Do you remember when we talked about that when I was demonstrating writing some pages a few days ago?"

"Yes, but I forgot about it when I was writing."

"It's not easy to remember when you are working hard writing the book, but I think it is a strategy that really works. Maybe sometimes you can read your work to a friend when we turn and share."

(*Turn and share* is a technique we use during writing workshop. The students take a break from their nearly silent writing and turn to another student at their table and read, explain, or share a part of their story. Writers get feedback and check the meaning of their text.)

"I also have a question about a couple of your illustrations. You did a great job drawing the cat and the rug on page 3, when she lost her ball of yarn, and a terrific job showing the cat chasing the catnip toy on page 9. I can see the cat and what's going on in both pictures. I wonder what the rest of the room might look like, though. If you were going to draw the indoor scene, what would you include?"

Sophia thinks a minute. "I would put the ball of yarn in the first picture and maybe a couch and some chairs."

"Is there a room in your house you are thinking of?"

"Yeah, the living room."

"Good idea. Do you think you may want to add that in your final draft?"

"Yes."

"On page 9, too?"

"Yes, 'cause that's the pattern in the book."

"Right. I think a bit more detail in the illustration on this page will help your audience get more meaning from your story. Another strategy is to draw a close-up picture of just the cat playing with the catnip toy. I think either way would work." (We have covered close-ups earlier in the year during drawing instruction. Sophia has practiced drawing close-ups in her sketchbook, so we have a common understanding of that technique.) I also ask her to consider a personal connection between her work and her life as a pet owner: "Is this the way your cat plays with a catnip toy?"

"Yes. He throws it all over the place."

"Yeah, I had a cat that did that, too. What is your cat's catnip toy made of?"

"Cloth, I think."

"I'll look forward to seeing what you choose to do with this picture, Sophia."

I move on to find out whether she wants to adjust the meaning on the hermit crab page. "I love your hermit crab's face, Sophia. It is really funny the way the eyes bug out. I have a quick question about his shell. I know it is taller than the old shell so he has more room to move around in it. That's all good. I'm wondering if there is another cool thing about the shell that you might want to mention in your writing."

Sophia looks at the picture and immediately says, "It's really colorful."

"It *is* colorful. Do you think you want to put that in?"

She nods.

"What words do you think you could add that would make sense?"

"What if I wrote 'a bigger, more colorful shell'?"

"That works really well," I say and watch as she makes the changes on her draft.

I have one more question. "Here on page 10, you say the owner gave the horse a 'better shoe than ever before.' You know a lot about horses, and I was wondering if you could tell me what you think the horse might do with that new shoe? I remember the bird in Kevin's story flew higher than he ever had before, and the shark in my story swam deeper than she ever had before. What could your horse do?"

She thinks. "Trot better than before?"

"Good thinking. Do you want to put that in?"

"OK." She makes the revision.

Then I remember her asking me for help with drawing the garden, and I turn to the last page. "How do you like the way the garden turned out?"

"Good, but I think I'll make it more of a trapezoid shape in my final draft." This floors me. She is using a concept from math pattern block work to augment her illustration. "I might make it bigger, too."

"That sounds good," I say. Sophia is taking control her of illustrations and the meaning they add to the story. I'm delighted.

I move on to the editing portion of the conference. "You are spelling all the sounds in the words you write, and I can read your writing easily. Let's see . . . you picked out the word *found* as one you had misspelled, and you were right. *Found* is spelled *f-o-u-n-d*. It contains the *ound* phonogram, along with *hound, sound, round, ground,* and all those guys. The *ound* phonogram is a pretty good one to learn, so let's add that to your words-to-learn book."

"OK," Sophia says and gets out the book. We find the *F* section and add *found* to it. She then goes back and corrects *found* each time it appears in her draft.

We repeat this process for *shoe*. Here, I focus on the meaning. "When you wrote *horse shoe*, you added a *w* to *sho* and wrote *horse show*. You've been to a horse show, haven't you? Here's an example of a spelling mistake changing the meaning of a story, huh? I knew what you meant because your picture and the rest of the words were so clear."

We also add *bigger* to her spelling book and discuss doubling ending consonants when adding a suffix like *er*. She makes the changes in her draft and also takes care of a few capitalization and punctuation miscues.

The piece is ready to be published. "You said you wanted to redo your illustrations, Sophia?" I ask.

"Yes, I think I can do a better job."

"Why don't we type up your story with the revisions and edits we made and you can take the final copy home and do the illustrations as homework?" I suggest.

"OK."

"Why don't you take one more look through and see whether there are any words you want to change before we give it to Maggie to type." (Maggie is an aide, or "helping teacher," who uses some of her time to type the children's stories.)

Including my own preparation time and meeting with each individual student, this kind of conferring may seem quite intensive. I realize when I write down every step, it seems like it takes more time than it actually does. My preparation time is actually about ten minutes per meeting, and each individual conference rarely exceeds fifteen minutes even with the deepest revision and edit. The conferences roll along like a good conversation—writers talking about writing. And it is all well worth the effort, as you can see from the type of work that is realized by each writer. This type of conferring, like any teaching, takes some ramping up. My expectations of myself have increased from when I started ten years ago. I also don't start the year with these types of conferences. They generally occur two or three times a year, when we roll out a new genre such as memoir, nonfiction, or fiction. In between, we continue to write, but the conferences are shorter and my preparation time is less intense.

I move on to confer with another child, and soon writing workshop comes to an end. When I check in with Sophia, I find she has added, "Little kitten found a catnip mouse made of cloth," on page 9. She hands in her draft, and Maggie types it that afternoon using a homemade computer template she and I have devised. Sophia takes the pages with her when she leaves for home.

She completes her illustrations that afternoon and evening, making several changes based on our conference conversations, my classroom demonstrations, and her own artistic license. Her completed piece is shown on pages 81–84.

On her cover, Sophia has switched the animal character pictures to iconic representations of the objects the characters found. This is a unique choice that neither Henkes nor I modeled. Sophia has taken the work to the next level; within the context of a comfortable and well-understood structure, she has stepped beyond the template into originality.

On page 1, Sophia has added the rainstorm picture that she suggested when I was demonstrating this strategy.

In her revised page 2 illustration, Sophia has changed the direction the horse is facing, simplified the picture to focus on the story action, and hidden the horseshoe behind the tree. She retains her layering of the figures, foliage, and clouds. She indicates the character's confusion with the cartoony question mark and shows his mood with a frown. Rain appears to be falling on the character and can also be seen behind the crown of the tree.

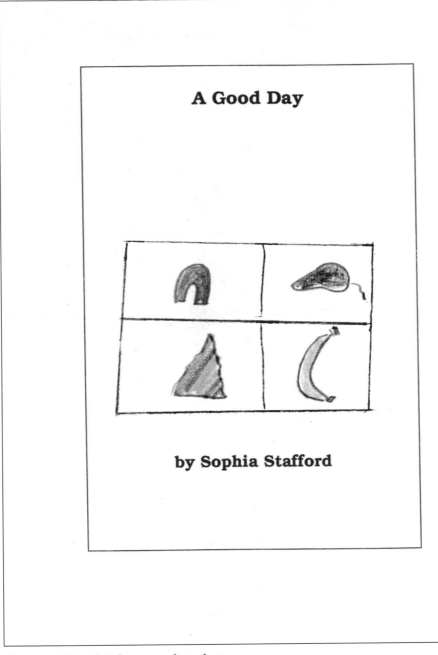

A Good Day

by Sophia Stafford

Cover of Sophia's completed story

It was a bad day.

-1-

Little horse lost his horseshoe.

-2-

"A Good Day" by Sophia Stafford *(continued)*

Kitten lost his ball of yarn.

-3-

Little hermit crab grew out of his shell.

-4-

Monkey lost his little banana.

-5-

But then...

-6-

"A Good Day" by Sophia Stafford *(continued)*

Little monkey found a bigger, tastier banana.

-7-

Little hermit crab moved in a bigger, more colorful shell.

-8-

"A Good Day" by Sophia Stafford *(continued)*

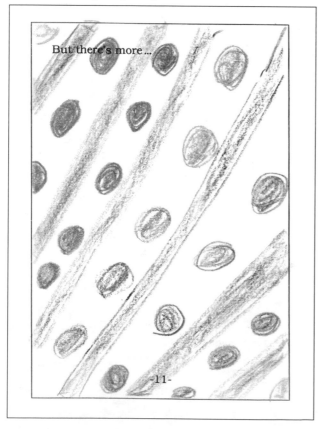

Sophia has brilliantly revised this picture on page 3 to enhance the meaning of the page. The cat reclines on the couch, confused about the lost ball of yarn, which sits on the windowsill. Outside the window, bad weather still sets the mood. There is chaos in the house as a ball flies in from off-frame left and heads for a fragile vase on a skinny table; an unknown grown-up sets limits from off-frame right. The cat is centered within the action. The result of Sophia's revision is a more inviting and satisfying reading experience for her audience.

Sophia has made slight revisions to this text on page 4, cleaning up the meaning and syntax. She has substituted a plastic log for the ocean, getting the idea from items in her home hermit crab aquarium. This is a great example of children blending ideas from their personal experience into their fiction. It provides a touch of realism that gives fiction credibility. The talk balloon helps us understand the hermit crab's state of mind, while the weather remains somber, replacing the sunshine in the draft.

Sophia has completely remade page 5, incorporating ideas we discussed in the revising conference about close-ups. We were talking about another picture then, but Sophia has applied the strategies to show the tears of sadness of the monkey who lost his little banana. The monkey's face fills nearly the entire frame. The tears are prominent, as is the frown highlighting his plight. Again she has revised the weather from the draft. Sophia has taken considerable care in composing this picture. She shows only part of the monkey's face, and the clouds dissolve behind his head at the top of the frame.

The first part of her story concluded, Sophia moves on to the transitional page introducing the section of the book in which all her characters' problems will be solved.

She uses the symbol of the sun and the improving weather I demonstrated to take us to act two.

On page 7 Sophia uses a slightly higher ground line, removes her clouds, and changes the monkey's pose to include hands on hips. A smaller sun rides high in the sky. Sophia has also deleted her talk balloon, perhaps feeling that the monkey's attitude and confidence are evident in his body language. The giant banana, planted in the green hill, is hilarious.

On page 8 the revised text is reflected in her illustration. The shell is taller and bigger, as it was in the first draft, but is now patterned and colored with considerable care and detail. Sophia has used colors in the shell that complement and bring out the colors in the landscape. The hermit crab is centered on the sloping hill in the foreground, between the abandoned shell in the extreme right background and the plastic log in the left foreground, with a high sun riding overhead in a blue sky. All is well for the hermit crab: he's smiling all over.

Sophia has reworked the drawing on page 9 to include more detail. The cat has moved off the couch and is launching the cloth catnip mouse high into the air and leaping after it (she's also smiling). The couch and the ball, inactive, anchor the drawing in the center, flanked by the cat and mouse on the left and the curtained window framing the bright sun on the right, with the ball of string cleverly positioned on the windowsill.

Sophia has revised the drawing on page 10 by centering the horse to show his total body, including his happy smile. She has revised the talk balloons as well, eliminating the horse's and changing the owner's to a reassuring "All right." She has raised her ground line and shifted the sun to the opposite side of the frame, creating a more balanced composition.

Bringing her story to a close, Sophia has added a second transitional drawing to carry us from the second part to the third part, featuring the surprise.

Her bright stripes and polka dots are similar to the stripes Henkes uses in his first two transitional pages, but Sophia has done something completely original by including this page, which neither Henkes nor I have done. She has decided one is needed and has added it.

On her final page, Sophia has kept her text intact and made slight revisions to the drawing—enlarging the clouds and shifting the sun from the left to the right. She has changed the shape of the garden to a trapezoid and also has included a digging tool. The words in the talk balloon are altered from "Look, Mom," to "Mom, Mom." The child looks slightly more like Sophia than the child in the draft.

Sophia has brought all her considerable writing and illustrating skills to this final product. Her drawings are thoughtful and carefully composed. Each illustration augments the meaning of the words on the page. Sophia has followed Henkes' text pattern, substituting animals that she knows and loves and social situations she is familiar with to create a unique story. Her understanding of hermit crabs, her love of horses, and her experience with gardening (and indoor ball playing) are all reflected in her work. She has applied her sharp artist's eye and sure, steady hand in her version of *A Good Day*.

Sophia has done what good writers do. She's used the ideas shared in drawing lessons and applied each idea with a generous dollop of originality, bringing her own twist to it. Her use of the close-up to show the emotion of the monkey is particularly effective. Sophia also uses her sense of humor in this story. Her drawings are funny and help us understand and appreciate her characters. It is easy to root for such simple yet well-developed heroes.

Sophia clearly understands the way Henkes' book works and can use this innovation experience to help her move on to other, more complex fiction structures. Her ability to weave simple lines of carefully chosen text with rich and vibrant illustrations, just like Henkes does, will serve her well in the future. He has been a good mentor to her, and I think he would be proud of how she honored his idea.

Another Take: Avery's Version of *A Good Day*

Now let's look at the way Avery handles this innovation. Avery is younger than Sophia, in her fourth month of first grade. With two older brothers, Avery is an independent thinker, but she relies on and expects good friends and family to help her when she is unsure how to proceed with reading, writing, and drawing. It is not unusual for her to ask a friend to help her draw a particular animal or spell a particular word. That's OK. Our writing workshop allows children to apprentice each other as well as published authors and me.

Avery has followed the lead of Kevin Henkes for her cover. It conveys the necessary information to introduce us to her four main characters.

On page 1, Avery follows the provided template to set the mood with troubled weather. She centers her cloud and fills the frame with raindrops.

Avery has a pet bunny, so it is natural and expected for a white bunny with a fluffy tail to show up in her story. Avery's text is

A Good Day

by Avery Jackson

It was a bad day.

-1-

"A Good Day" by Avery Jackson

Bunny lost her fur.

-2-

Pig couldn't find his mud.

-3-

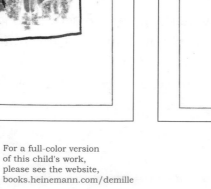

For a full-color version
of this child's work,
please see the website,
books.heinemann.com/demille

Dog lost his bone.

-4-

Cat lost her kitten.

-5-

"A Good Day" by Avery Jackson *(continued)*

But then.

-6-

Cat looked behind her and she found her kitten playing.

-7-

Dog dug up a bigger bone.

-8-

Bunny grew more fur.

-9-

"A Good Day" by Avery Jackson *(continued)*

But there's more. . . .

-10-

A little girl found a piece of fur and shouted, "Mom it's a good day!".

-11-

simple and cut to the bone, and at her stage of development, this is what should be expected and accepted. Goals for Avery are different from those for Sophia. Avery is just learning this fiction pattern and has had less experience with telling, writing, and illustrating stories, so her book does not contain the added description that Henkes and Sophia have provided. Last year, Sophia's writing had much in common with Avery's. Time spent writing, reading, and discussing quality fiction and unpacking the strategies of authors; drawing instruction; and personal interest, initiative, and talent have all blended to make Sophia the storyteller and writer she is today. Avery is on a similar path.

I have demonstrated how to make a pig earlier in the year. Avery has practiced drawing the pig in her sketchbook and has reproduced the animal (sporting an ornate and curly tail) as the second character in her book. Her drawing of the mud and water mixed together is a window into her literal way of thinking. To make mud, you need dirt and water, so to *draw* mud, you need blue for water and brown for dirt—if you mix the colors, you get mud. Avery has clearly communicated in words and pictures on page 3.

Avery's dog unsuccessfully looks for his bone. Avery once more sticks with animals she has had experience drawing; the dog is another animal we've all practiced together. She again writes a short sentence with no added description, keeping her text consistent from page to page.

The first portion of the story closes with Avery's cat character searching for her lost kitten. Avery has assigned the male gender to the dog and pig, the female gender to the cat and bunny.

Avery uses the demonstrated transition page showing the improving weather to introduce the section of her book in which the characters' problems will be solved. This transition page reminds emerging writers that the tone will now change and helps scaffold this writing experience.

The drawing on page 7, with mother and child reunited, a tiny golden sun sparkling between them, brought Avery's mother to tears. The kitten balances one paw on a ball of yarn, and each character's face seems to be smiling in contentment. Avery's drawing has begun to express rich story details before her text writing has. This is why teaching the fundamentals of drawing is an important tool in helping students craft quality literature.

Avery solves the dog's problem with a large cartoon bone he has dug up, and she shares a describing detail. This bone could only be characterized as bigger. She describes objects in the most literal way, which is consistent with her stage of development.

The bunny grows more fur to replace the missing spot. She sits on a high horizon line. Avery has included the tiny sun (visible on all pages of the problem-solving section).

Avery, like Sophia, includes a transitional page in her book to introduce the last section, in which the child gets the gift from the animal. She decorates it with several of her favorite colors in a bright patterned arrangement of dots, lines, and swirls.

On her final page, Avery has depicted the girl holding the bunny's fur and shouting to her mom. It is her largest drawing, featuring a full frame, a green rolling hill, blue sky, and a multicolored house. Mom is presumably inside the house. The fur is fully visible in the girl's hand. This is another example of Avery's ability to tell a more detailed story in pictures than in writing.

Avery is on a path toward providing more details in both her drawings and her text. Even in the course of this one story, her illustrations show evidence of developing details. She has made good use of drawing demonstrations, her story plan, the structure of the Henkes book, and suggestions and tips from table partners to create her own unique take on *A Good Day*.

Matching students with quality mentor texts, reading the books to them, unpacking the unique and special skills and strategies of the authors, scaffolding writing experiences, revising and editing interesting and exciting literature with emerging writers, and bringing inspired original pieces of literature to publication are what I get to do each day during writing workshop. It is hard work. It is also a pleasure and an honor to watch this work get done.

In Chapter 5 we'll look at how two students innovate a classic Arnold Lobel story.

Apprenticing with Arnold Lobel

I love Arnold Lobel's books. His unpretentious, amusing, and poignant stories won him both Newbery and Caldecott medals. He had a particular gift for creating memorable characters. His most famous characters, Frog and Toad, explore friendship in a realistic and hilarious way. Lobel's work, like Jim Henson's Muppets, operates on two creative levels—one is easily accessible to children; the other exudes a deeper, more sophisticated humor and poignancy appreciated by adults. One of the reasons his stories continue to be so popular is that both children and adults find deep resonance and spiritual meaning in them. Lobel was trained as a graphic illustrator and didn't consider himself much of a writer, but he had been telling stories all his life. He said once on his website, "I know how to draw pictures. With writing, I really don't know what I'm doing. It's very intuitive." Lobel is most worthy of an author study.

Mouse Tales (1972) is one of my primary-grade students' favorite books. A mouse father (modeled on Lobel himself) tells a bedtime tale to each of his seven children. One of these tales, "The Old Mouse," is well loved by every class I've ever had. Early in my teaching career, I used this story to entice my students to read *Mouse Tales* and the other Lobel Easy Readers. But it took me several years to understand how useful the story would be for teaching writing.

Old Mouse, the cranky surrogate adult in the story, can't stand the young mice. He avoids them on his morning walk and calls them harsh and hateful names when he sees them. Then one day his suspenders break and he loses his pants. This never fails to bring gales of laughter from my young listeners. Realizing he is in a jam, Old Mouse appeals to his usual support systems, other adult mice. Two ladies about his age freak out at his appearance, and his wife responds by telling him he looks silly in his underwear and bonking him on the head with a rolling pin. This brings on more laughter from the audience, as any mention of underwear in the classroom is bound to. Old Mouse hits bottom at this point and begins to weep. The children mice, seeing his predicament, respond by showing him the compassion and kindness that he never showed them. They give him love even when some would say he doesn't warrant it. The young mice come up with an ingenious repair: they use bubblegum to hold his pants up—a brilliant solution. Old Mouse's pants never fall down again, and more important, he gains a new admiration and affection for the children mice. He is transformed.

This is the classic redemption story, a favorite theme in literature. It is brilliantly told in six brief, elegant, and accessible pages. It is initially attractive to young readers because of the slapstick humor. Children are also drawn to the heroic nature of the young mice and their willingness to overlook the shortcomings and prejudices of Old Mouse, turn the other cheek, and help him when he is in need. The young mice do the right thing. Lobel also includes interesting and effective vocabulary and the unconventional use of bubblegum to hold up Old Mouse's pants, which makes total sense to primary students.

The advantages of this story as a mentor text are many.

First, it is brief. The entire story covers six 5-by-3 $1/2$ inch pages: 131 words in all, with illustrations. It is a quick, satisfying read.

Second, it has an effective structure that is easy to unpack and explain and is simple for primary-age writers to understand and get their minds around. There is a brief and clear introduction of a main character who immediately announces his aversion to children in the harsh dialogue with which he addresses them: no burying of the lead. This is followed by a story problem that has no doubt been pleasing audiences since pants were invented. After losing his pants, Old Mouse seeks help and is rebuffed by those who should help him, whereupon he bottoms out in tears. This allows the audience to develop a shade of compassion for Old

Mouse, even though he is a curmudgeon. At this point the children mice respond with kindness and the ingenious bubblegum solution, and Old Mouse is redeemed: a happy ending.

Third, the characters are well sketched and compelling without going overboard: Lobel says just enough to serve the story.

Fourth, the story has an effective arc that motivates emotional involvement even though the subject matter is ridiculous.

Fifth, the message is instructive and positive. Lobel at his best is a modern-day Aesop. This story is cut from the same cloth as the classic fables. The message of reaching out and helping those in need is important and timeless.

Last, the redemption story is a classic archetype that children will come in contact with numerous times as they read more widely and deeply. Understanding Lobel's patterns and structures will help them have deeper comprehension and an increased understanding of this type of fiction.

After I read the story aloud to the class once or twice, we work as a large group to develop a brief one- or two-sentence summary.

Then I lead a discussion of the structure, or parts, of the story. As the discussion progresses, I record on chart paper or an overhead transparency the parts we identify, like this:

"The Old Mouse," by Arnold Lobel

A redemption or change-of-heart story

SUMMARY: An old mouse who hates children changes his mind about them when they help him solve an embarrassing problem.

The story has six parts:
1. It begins with an introduction that features harsh dialogue.
2. An unexpected problem occurs.
3. People who usually help the old mouse don't—slapstick humor, the mouse is moved to tears.
4. The children mice have compassion and come to the rescue.
5. They solve the problem in a clever way.
6. Happy ending—the old mouse changes his attitude.

After the students have a solid understanding of the structure of this story, they are ready to use it as a model for their own fiction pieces. I've approached this using three different templates.

The first I call *The Old Mouse* planning page. It starts out with a prompt, then restates the information the class developed about the structure or parts of the story:

The Old Mouse *Planning Page*

A redemption or change-of-heart story

WHAT TO DO: Write a story like "The Old Mouse," but change the characters to animals you know and love. In your story,

1. your main character should reveal whom he or she hates through harsh dialogue;
2. an unexpected problem should happen;
3. characters who usually help the main character won't (include slapstick humor, and have character show sadness);
4. the hated characters should have compassion and come to the rescue;
5. they should solve the problem in a clever way; and
6. there should be a happy ending—your main character should change his mind about the characters he once hated.

This template breaks down Lobel's model and asks students to use their own knowledge of animals and situations and construct a story that resembles "The Old Mouse" but is unique to them. Innovating on Lobel, these writers use the same strategies a master writer has employed to construct award-winning, classic literature. They are not copying or plagiarizing but creating an innovated text based on a proven and effective structure and incorporating literary devices that are known to work with an audience—in this case, slapstick humor, well-sketched characters, an effective story arc, surprising and unexpected character responses, clever problem solving, and character redemption. My students enter into a long-distance apprenticeship with Lobel, learning how he approached one of his stories and then trying it themselves based on what they know and love. I also ask them to publish their manuscripts, so there is a real outcome of the work that begins with hearing the story, unpacking the structure, and employing what they know to write their own stories.

An alternative template recasts the same information as a questionnaire:

Lobel Story Questionnaire

Answer the questions below to help plan your redemption or change-of-heart story like Arnold Lobel's "The Old Mouse."

1. What animal will your main character be?

   _____

2. What opposing animal will your main character hate?

   _____

3. What harsh dialogue will your main character use to show how much he or she hates the opposing characters?

   _____

   _____

4. What animals will refuse to help your character? What funny things will happen to your character?

   _____

   _____

5. How will your main character show sadness?

   _____

   _____

6. How will the hated characters show kindness and come to the rescue?

   _____

   _____

7. What clever way will they solve the main character's problem?

   _____

   _____

8. How will your story end? How will you show your main character has changed his or her mind about the once-hated characters?

   _____

   _____

Some primary writers need further scaffolding in order to complete this task. In that case I use a third template, a table like this:

Main Character	Characters the Main Character Hates	Unexpected Problem for Main Character	Characters That Should Help but Don't	How the Hated Characters Come to the Rescue	Happy Ending

When each column in the table is filled with information in the form of words or pictures, the writer will have the information needed to create a redemption story.

Use one of these templates only if you need to. Many children will be able to go right from the large-group-determined story structure to a draft of a six-page stapled-down-the-side book. You'll quickly identify the writers who may benefit from using an organizer.

Colin's Innovation

Colin is a curly-headed first grader with a great sense of humor and a love for comic strips. He regularly quotes Calvin and Hobbes, and his cartoon-inspired sound effects accompany much of our classroom day. Colin spends a great deal of time on the water with his family. A highlight of his year is traveling to Matinicus Rock off the coast of Maine and participating in the annual puffin count. Colin enjoys reading nonfiction, including books about Maine mammals that he has encountered (or wishes he had encountered) during family camping trips. Here's Colin's reworking of Lobel's book, with my commentary. The story is titled *Help from a Hater* (he chose not to use a template).

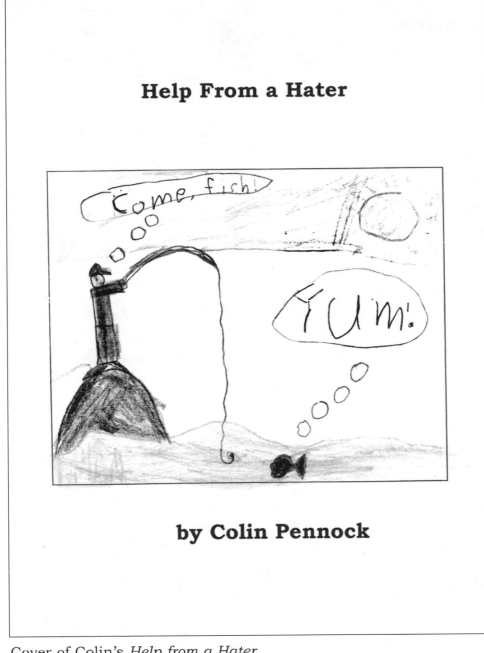

Help From a Hater

by Colin Pennock

Cover of Colin's *Help from a Hater*

For a full-color version of this child's work, please see the website, books.heinemann.com/demille

Colin's cover illustration foreshadows the fate of his main character, a technique employed by many of the authors Colin has read.

On page 1, Colin identifies two animals he knows about, a fish and a bear, as his main and hated characters. He writes a swift and effective lead and makes meaningful use of a cartoon technique—a hate cloud—to let the reader in on what the fish is thinking.

One time a fish swam along, yelling at bears, and simply hating them.

1

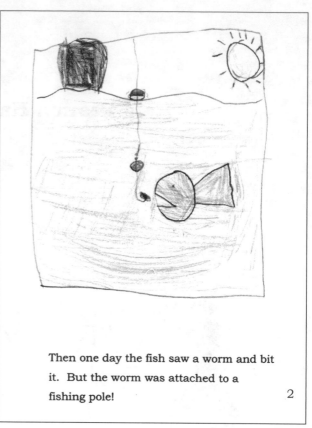

Then one day the fish saw a worm and bit it. But the worm was attached to a fishing pole!

2

Colin's *Help from a Hater (continued)*

"HELP!!" he cried. A swordfish came and said, "Too bad, Bozo!"

3

JERK!! Up and out of the water he went.

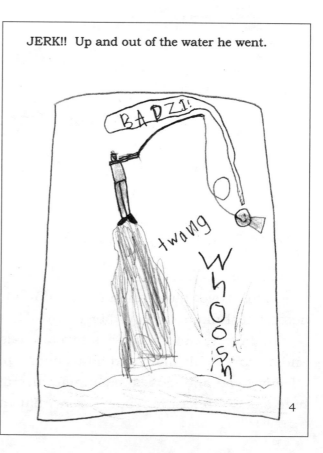

4

A sea turtle crawled by saying, "So long, sucker!"

5

On pages 2 and 3, Colin establishes his story problem effectively and dramatically. Once more his illustrations ably augment the text. He closes in on the action on page 2 to let us see the fish with an open mouth about to bite the worm. He then widens the shot on page 3 to reveal the fisherman landing his catch. Liberal use of onomatopoeia lets us in on the action.

On pages 4 and 5, Colin uses more information garnered from comic books and other pop culture sources. The phrases "Too bad, bozo" and "So long, sucker" fit perfectly into Lobel's structure: these characters are not going to be helpful and the fish is on his own.

On pages 6 and 7, Colin resolves the story: the bear comes to the rescue, knocking the fisherman into the water, and the

Colin's *Help from a Hater (continued)*

When a bear came he said, "I'll save you!" He leaped on the fisherman knocking him into the water and setting the fish free.

6

From then on the fish loved bears.

7

captive fish gets his freedom back. Comic-book techniques again are used: a talk balloon, more onomatopoeia, and a "love" heart glowing next to a brilliant red sun (a happy accident perhaps, but a touch that warms and brightens the happy ending). Tragedy is narrowly averted.

Colin has used Lobel's model to create a piece of literature that stands on its own. Weaving in animals he knows and loves, writing strategies he has learned from storybooks he has read, language from popular culture, and comic-strip techniques that support and augment meaning, he has built on Lobel's original idea. Colin has included all the significant elements of fiction that Lobel uses in his story. He assimilates and reuses the structure of the story but breaks the boundaries to include supporting elements that make his story unique to his own experience. Colin can now include fiction among the types of writing he has completed and is on the way toward mastering.

Helena's Innovation

Helena is a friendly second grader with an easy grin, a strong flair for the dramatic, and a mischievous sense of humor. She has had more experience with fiction than Colin has: she's a natural storyteller and has probably read thousands of books so far in her lifetime. She is also a talented artist who has spent countless hours with pencils, markers, crayons, and paper. She has a brilliant imagination and a direct connection to the absurd. Helena loves animals, has a variety of pets at home, and is crazy about horses.

Before writing *The Mischievous Kitten*, Helena organized her story using the scaffolding table:

Main Character	Characters the Main Character Hates	Unexpected Problem for Main Character	Characters That Should Help but Don't	How the Hated Characters Come to the Rescue	Happy Ending
little kitten	mice	falls in full bathtub	soap bar and drain plug	dove into the tub and pulled out the plug	kitten takes mice with her everywhere she goes . . . friends forever

She chose to use the table for the following reasons, even though she is an experienced writer:

- personal choice
- she has a deeper understanding of the value of such a tool
- she is a more patient and organized student than some
- her friends were doing it at her writing table

The Mischievous Kitten

Look at that!

by Helena Solorzano

Once there was a little kitten who loved to explore. Each morning she would meet her worst enemies, the mice. When they popped out she said, "Back you horrid thieves!"

Run away

Helena's story

For a full-color version of this child's work, please see the website, books.heinemann.com/demille

On page 1, Helena introduces her characters much like Lobel does, with a short lead. She includes effective describing, naming, and action words—*worst, enemies,* and *popped*. She also includes harsh dialogue to indicate the kitten's hatred of the mice. Her illustration shows the kitten in a human pose and uses a talk balloon to convey the mice's reaction.

One day she went into the bathroom.
She jumped into the bathtub. She
didn't know it was full of water. She
couldn't get out and she couldn't swim.

She said, "Help Soap Bar!". "No way,
you're a cat!", said Soap Bar. She went
underwater and gurgled, "Help!" gurgle,
"me!". "No!" gurgle "way!" gurgled the
plug. The chain on the plug gave her a
tap on the nose.

The kitten started to cry.

Helena introduces the problem

On page 2, Helena introduces her problem effectively. Understanding a kitten's natural curiosity and hatred of water, she has the kitten mistakenly jump into a full bathtub. Recently Sarah, a classmate, shared a similar event during a storytelling session. Helena's drawing of the bathtub reveals excellent perspective, an impressive horizon line, and an accurate mouse hole and seems to have been influenced by Garth Williams' *Stuart Little* illustrations. She is also borrowing from a scene in a chapter book I have recently read aloud, *Toys Go Out*, by Emily Jenkins, in which a stuffed animal gets stuck in a bathtub. Her talk balloon adds to the growing tension and highlights the predicament of the kitten. She then personifies the soap bar and the drain plug as potential helpers. Drawing from her own experiences and popular culture film references, she adds the effective (and hilarious) "gurgle, gurgle" details of the kitten and chain's underwater conversation. Using the Lobel technique of revealing that the character has hit bottom (this time literally), she ends the page with the single line "The kitten started to cry."

The mice saw and heard the kitten's cries.
"We have to help her!", yelled the mice.
"Lashalies to the rescue!" said a mouse.
They dived into the tub and together pulled up the plug. They drained the water. The kitten was shivering in a corner. All the Lashalies dragged a warm towel over and wrapped it around the kitten.

Helena's page 3

Resolution is close at hand on page 3. Helena mobilizes her mouse crew and provides them with an amusing rallying cry—the last name of the mice family. Her solution is innovative and brave. The mice show extra compassion by wrapping the kitten in a towel, a detail that is certainly drawn from Helena's own experience. More talk balloons—Helena includes a shivery "Thank you" from the kitten and a jaunty "No prob!" from the mice—augment the text.

The story concludes with a charming illustration of the kitten transporting the three mice on her back and the assertion that the kitten and the mice were friends forever.

Helena, like Colin, adheres to the structure of Lobel's original story but takes it in her own direction based on her unique writing abilities and interests. Her adapted story, filled with wit and charm,

Whenever the kitten went to explore she
took the mice with her.

They were friends forever!

Helena's happy ending

works on its own as a piece of second-grade literature. She has
picked main characters—the kitten and the mice—that she knows
well and can illustrate effectively. To create a plausible and compelling problem, she incorporates an experience in a story she
heard a classmate tell. To make the bathtub sequence more realistic, she personifies (to great effect) inanimate objects that would be
present in a bathtub. She draws from influences beyond Lobel,
including movie references (the "gurgle, gurgle" dialogue), rallying
cries ("Lashalies to the rescue!"), personal experiences (being
wrapped cozily in a towel), and knowledge of book illustrators (her
Garth Williams–esque drawings).

———

Helena and Colin have done much more than copy Lobel's story.
They used "The Old Mouse" as a starting point and drew inspira-

tion from this classic tale. They studied the story and assimilated the structure and the fundamental elements that make it a good read. They then used that structure as the outline for their own original stories. While writing, they reinvented the original tale with new information from their own experiences as readers, writers, moviegoers, comic-book aficionados, animal lovers, artists, video game players, and members of the human race. The stories they crafted indicate an understanding of the elements of fiction they learned from their long-distance apprenticeship with Lobel. They have also learned that what they bring to the story through their own individuality is just as important.

Even at this early stage you can see each of their voices emerging. They can't help writing what they know, what they have experienced, and what and whom they love. Helena and Colin (along with the rest of my first and second graders) have learned how to craft a redemption story. They have used the structure and fundamentals of Lobel's model to write entertaining pieces of literature.

In addition, both children have started to absorb and make use of the key elements of fiction. Let's look more closely at just what those key elements of fiction are as we turn our attention to the mother of all fiction genres: the fairy tale.

6
CHAPTER

Introducing Fairy Tales

$\mathcal{W}$hen my students begin writing original fairy tales, I get even more specific about the underlying structure of fiction stories. In doing our innovations on mentor authors, we have already begun thinking about the ingredients of successful narratives. Now, as we enter the world of fairy tales, we challenge ourselves to be even more conscious about using all the tools in the storyteller's repertoire.

The Seven Elements of Fiction

Fiction, like all genres, has a basic structure. Without structure, children's stories have to rely solely on charm and energy, which can result in a lack of clarity and point. Too much structure and adult intervention, and the entire class' fairy tales will be one-dimensional, with grown-up fingerprints visible all over them. So what to do? What do young writers need to know? How much structure is enough, and what elements of fiction are helpful and teachable to primary students?

In my classroom, I distill the elements down to seven ingredients that young writers need to include to craft effective and interesting pieces of fiction. These are the same elements we encounter as adult readers of novels. In class, I teach the actual terms and use connecting language and metaphors to help children understand how each element plays an important part in a made-up story. When we are reading a fairy tale or any fictional story, we see whether we can identify each element. When we are writing our own tales, we make certain we've included each element, even if it is just one sentence. I've noticed again and again that if a piece of writing is not working, it is usually because one of these seven elements has been left out or underwritten.

You can teach these elements to kids in plain, simple language, using examples from the storybooks they know and love the best. When they see that their favorite authors—Kevin Henkes, Joy Cowley, Maurice Sendak, Arnold Lobel—all use these same ingredients, they are eager to try them out in their own stories.

The Lead

The lead is often included as part of the plot, but I believe it is important enough to teach it to beginning fiction writers as a distinct element. A story has to have an inviting and interesting beginning: that's the purpose of the lead, which can take many different forms. It can be mysterious, traditional, or comic. Good leads can consist of dialogue or description and can even contain other elements of fiction, such as character attributes or details about the setting. A lead can ease us into the story or get the reader's heart racing. A good lead is an invitation to enter the world of the writer. It makes a strong first impression for the rest of the piece. The lead is where the story starts.

A Description of the Setting

Describing the setting is essential if you want your readers to melt into the story and enter the reading zone. They have to be able to imagine where the story is taking place, where the characters are living and interacting. An effective description of the setting works in harmony with the illustrations in a storybook or fairy tale to captivate readers. The right amount of detail and the right tone are key, as are the link from the lead and the link to the main character. The description of the setting needn't be particularly long, but it has to evoke the world the characters live in; the audience must see clearly the white farmhouse, the large red barn, and the trickling stream running down by the old stone wall. Sensory language is a good tool to use. What do we see? Hear? Feel? Smell? Good setting descriptions can be realized through colorful, detailed drawings.

The Introduction and Description of the Main Character

Characters are the driving force of fiction. We relate to the characters. We see ourselves in them and try to understand what motivates them. Without good characters, we have difficulty staying with a piece of writing no matter how much action is taking place. The better we can imagine a character in our mind, the better we'll enjoy the story.

Physical descriptions can also dictate how we feel about characters—whether we have confidence in them or feel sorry for them, how well we like them, and how much we root for them. Effective description covers not only what the characters look like but also how they act and how they are viewed by their communities. We are interested in whether they are well liked, underestimated, or given a free ride. The description of a character can shed light on her essence, the quality of her personality, and even what is in her soul.

The Problem

So what's the problem? I ask primary-grade writers that question all the time. A key element in fiction is the problem the main character has to solve. Each story gets its juice from the disruption of harmony in the world the writer has created. Introducing the problem in a clever and interesting way creates delicious tension that readers can't resist sticking with. The problem—in concert with the lead, the setting, and the characters—sets up the story as a page-turner. There are many types of story problems, or conflicts. Most of the ones I encounter while teaching fiction and fairy tales pit the main character against an opposing character (protagonist versus antagonist) or against nature.

An opposing character needs to be described, usually in unflattering terms, before the problem is introduced. Readers need to know why they should dislike or even hate this character. What has this character done that puts him in conflict with the hero? Often the opposing character is evil, ugly, and unkind—the polar opposite of the hero. The more readers initially dislike the opposing character, the better the story works and the greater the tension and the drama that unfolds.

If the writer is crafting a main-character-against-nature problem, the description of the setting becomes more important. In these stories the main character has to fight the cruelties of nature and pass a number of tests (usually three) before reaching an ultimate goal. There may be rivers to cross, mountains to climb, and dark woods to go through before the hero finds a special jewel that will save the quiet village. The description of the setting and the ways the main character struggles to move through it determine how well the story works.

Another popular problem involves a transformation. In these stories, mermaids change into girls in order to seek their true loves or animals transform into people at full moon. These tales are filled with magic and difficult choices and often have surprising resolutions.

Often young writers' story problems borrow details directly or indirectly from stories by their favorite authors. Or their main characters may live out some kind of hope, wish, or dream in the company of other characters bearing the names of classmates or beloved teachers and family members. These stories can be windows into the hearts and minds of the writers.

The Rising Action

The rising action is the most difficult part of fiction for primary students to understand and therefore to tackle. Put simply, it is what happens to the main character between the establishment of the story problem and the beginning of the story resolution. In a quest story, it is where the hero is tested and encounters strange, comic, and oftentimes helpful supporting characters. During the rising action, the main character faces the problem, then uses her strength, wits, and good fortune to put together and carry out the plan that will restore harmony to her disrupted life. In the best fiction, there is a gradual and entertaining buildup to the story climax: information may be exchanged, lies told, the stage set for battle.

The Climax

The climax is where the rubber meets the road. It is the high point of the story—the ultimate action. If a story were a fever chart, it is the point where the temperature would peak. The evil character is vanquished; the hero finds the lost treasure; the dragon is slain; the troll is sent flying into the water, never to be heard from again; the key slides into the lock and the door is opened. Often the truth about evil characters and the truth about the hero's character, courage, and bravery are revealed at a story's climax. All roads lead to this moment.

The Ending and Resolution

The endings of stories written by primary-grade writers are almost always happy. Children model their fiction after the fairy tales and picture books they've read and that have been read to them, in which everything usually works out in the end. Justice is done. The hero is victorious, bad characters are taught a lesson, the problem is solved, and harmony is restored. Evil characters are often redeemed, usually by the kindness of the hero. This sweet and optimistic trait is a reminder that at this age, children are still generally hopeful and forgiving and view the world as a place where everything can work out and all people can be redeemed. I like that about them, and I like that about fiction.

But not all children write happy endings. Their life experiences dictate they way they approach fiction. They may act out their disappointments, fears, and insecurities in the pages of their stories. What they write is a window into their thoughts, hopes, wishes, and dreams—and also their anger, resentment, and despair. It will be up to you to decide appropriate limits for how far they should take their ideas. Consider the audience: if the intended audience is the kindergarten class, the story should probably have a happy ending and be less scary or graphic than if the audience is older children. Sometimes the decision will be made for you. Some schools have zero tolerance for stories with violence, weapons, any kind of graphic depiction. Discussions about how much is too much can be dizzying. I leave it to your good judgment to decide.

Writing Fairy Tales

My fairy tale unit combines reading and writing. I use the best fairy tales to point out the elements of fiction and show my students how authors use these elements. I read aloud, and the children read on their own, a wide variety of fairy tales and folktales. I typically read aloud and discuss two or three tales per day—stories I or the class really love and enjoy. I also read tales that demonstrate a particular element of fiction I'm trying to teach.

Once I've established the daily pattern of reading and discussing great fairy tales, I augment these stories with writing and drawing activities: identifying and crafting leads, noticing and describing story setting, considering and describing characters, revealing the essence of a character, imagining a character's back-story, mapping existing fairy tales and short fiction, identifying key story language, listing and evaluating tales we've read, and telling our own made-up stories. I introduce, describe, and model all of these activities in minilessons, and the children complete them during guided work periods.

As we continue to talk about setting, characters, and problems that would be interesting for audiences to read about, we make personal lists of settings, characters, and problems we might like to write about. I model what I've seen the students do a hundred times. I get six pieces of plain white paper, fold them in half, and staple them together in three spots along the left-hand side. Once I have built my book, I refer to my list of settings, characters, and problems; pick one setting and two characters; and dig in, right in front of the kids. I model starting with the lead on page 1. I write my lead and draw a corresponding picture. Then I model turning the page and continuing on page 2, where I delineate a small illustration box and draw a colorful setting. As I begin writing about my setting underneath the illustration, I may get to the end of the page and not be finished. I ask the students what I should do, and they tell me to go on to the next page. It's what professional authors do. Now they are chomping at the bit to get started themselves.

Assessing and Conferring

As the kids gather their materials and set to work, I circulate, observing, conferring, and coaching. I try to keep my assessment and feedback process simple. Shelley Harwayne (2002 lecture, Walloon Institute) reminds us that we are not in the big league of writing; we are in the little league. The child should remain in control of his story. Overrevise, and you take the story out of the child's hands and make it your own.

The purpose of this fairy tale study is to teach children the elements of fiction so they can express their creativity independently by writing stories. While the kids are writing, I look for elements of fiction that have been clearly written and examples of effective story language. I offer positive comments. I praise detailed and colorful illustrations that augment the text. I look for indications of emerging author voice and any other unique features that show the writer using what she knows and loves to make the story original.

I also look for and note elements of fiction that are absent (very few) and underwritten (slightly more) and ask questions about the author's intentions. What does the town your hero lives in look like? Can you describe how your character looks more clearly? Can you explain why the bad guy in your story is scary? What is your main character's problem with the bad guy? I write these questions down on sticky notes and prepare for conferences, just like I did with Sophia in Chapter 4. Sometimes elements of fiction are left out because the student does not understand or has not retained the information from the minilessons or the supplementary activities. The revision conference is a good second teaching opportunity. Sometimes students skip or underwrite an element because they are tired or distracted. Conferring gives me and the students a chance to see how they are doing with the work and ascertain what help they need to progress in attempting to write fairy tales for the first time.

Remember—try never to do too much in any one conference. Pay attention to what's most important at the moment. If the majority of the class is having difficulty with one of the elements, that's a red flag that you need to reteach that element in a minilesson, perhaps in a different way. How well you know each student as a person and a writer dictates how you proceed. Your manner, techniques, and how much you'll cover will vary based on the student you are working with and what that child responds to.

If children are good at revising text on their own, ask a question and talk a little about how they might answer it. Talk back and forth about a passage of description and then let them go back to work. If they need more room, they can make their revision on a sticky note and affix it to the page.

If children are not ready to make revisions independently, point out and discuss needed improvements and have them tell you what should be written down. As they speak, take dictation and record it in the appropriate spot.

In addition to revising for craft techniques, you'll also want to edit each piece of writing as it nears publication. Again, don't bite off more than you can chew or give each child more than he can handle. In my classroom, I plan a full range of activities that give students opportunities to practice spelling and other writing conventions. Together, we look for three or four spelling words per story to add to their words-to-learn list. We find places where punctuation (periods and question marks primarily) would help a reader make sense of the text. We also look for places where capital letters are warranted. As with revising, some children are able to complete editing tasks independently, while others need varying degrees of support.

When the students and I are satisfied with their stories, we move on to publishing. In my classroom, most fairy tales are published twice. The first appearance is a text-only version that goes into our school literary magazine, Acorns, which is published two or three times during the year. This version is read by the entire school community, and writers receive feedback from revered older students, friends, family, and classmates. The second publication is a fully illustrated, typed book. Classroom volunteers work with the students to produce a typed version incorporating all revisions and edits. Students have the option of redoing the illustrations, color photocopying the original art, or cutting and pasting the originals into the typed final copy. This final copy goes home to be enjoyed by the writer's family, and a photocopy is placed in the child's portfolio.

The primary aim of the fairy tale unit is to teach the elements of fiction so each child will eventually be able to create, independently, a story worthy of audience attention. A second goal is to create and preserve a community of writers. The process is modeled closely on how real writers work and how they support one another as they conceive ideas, create drafts, find and fix problems, and share their work.

Let's look at examples of original fairy tale, starting with Ella's stories.

7 CHAPTER

Helping Ella Write a Fairy Tale

One of my first graders wrote a simple but charming fairy tale during our midyear fairy tale unit. She had already tried a Kevin Henkes–inspired piece of fiction and written in the style of Dr. Seuss. Examining her process will give you a window into how this unit plays out in the classroom.

Ella is quite an independent thinker, which works both for and against her. When she decides she can do something, the sky is the limit, but when she thinks she can't, it is difficult to convince her otherwise. She has listened avidly to all the fairy tales I've read aloud and read many on her own but has a bit of trouble getting the elements of fiction under her belt as a writer.

She asks for many quick conferences while she writes her fairy tale. I accommodate these requests because I know her well and understand that she needs support in order to do her best work. With young writers who are trying a genre for the first time, many short conversations throughout the process help to both reassure them and nudge them along.

We start simply, by having a quick discussion about choosing characters and a setting. Ella picks a bunny for her protagonist (she has a pet bunny and has already written several memoirs about this relationship) and a dog as the opposing character. I ask her what a good setting might be and remind her that because it is a made-up story it can take place anywhere she imagines. She chooses Candyland, from the popular children's board game. Two elements down—the first hurdles have been successfully negotiated.

The creative process is often jump-started by something seen, heard, or felt. The artist or writer blends this outside information with what's going on in her conscious and subconscious mind and forms original ideas. Hearing a song or seeing something on the roadside while I'm driving has often spurred a song or story that I hadn't known I wanted to write.

Since I know Ella will need to visualize these elements in order to write about them, I suggest she draw her setting and her main characters in her sketchbook to get an idea of how they might look. This strategy is standard in my classroom: even for older and more experienced primary fiction writers, visualizing a setting and characters provides important information they can refer to when they are writing.

Drawing a character or a setting feeds the writer in two ways. First, a visualization is much easier for many primary writers to translate into a drawing than into words. The writer then has time to watch the settings and the characters emerge on paper. Young writers *see* their settings and characters coming to life like an old, slowly developing Polaroid photograph. As they draw, they are able to muse, think, talk, and create a plan for the story. Some of these ideas will eventually find their way into the story, and some will be rejected; this is simply the time for the ideas to be collected. Second, when the pictures are completed, they become a vital reference. It is easier to describe a character or a setting that you can lay your eyes on. The picture introduces the character and the setting to the writer, who can then list characteristics of both to include in the written story.

I know Ella's pictures will take her a while to create. I also know that while she is drawing, ideas for a story problem will begin to percolate. I leave her at her worktable to get started.

Sure enough, in a few minutes, she begins to talk softly to her tablemates about her main characters. "My bunny is magic," I overhear her say. "It has a magic wand." As she draws her opposing character, a bad dog, she says, "This dog is a robber." Later, as she begins her drawing of the setting, I hear her announce, "He lives in a candy house."

Here are her drawings of her setting and characters:

For a full-color version
of this child's work,
please see the website,
books.heinemann.com/demille

Ella's magic bunny

Her magic bunny has wings and a very prominent magic wand.

Ella's bad dog

The bad dog has his telltale bag of stolen loot.

The magic bunny's home is made of candy.

When I next check in with Ella, she is ready to begin her draft.
She decides she needs a twelve-page booklet, so we choose six
sheets of paper, fold them in half, and staple them together down

The magic bunny's house

the spine. Deciding to wait until she is a little more into the story before she chooses a title, she starts composing her lead.

Ella has information about the setting and the characters of her fairy tale but is perplexed about how to begin writing. She knows about leads from reading and listening to many fairy tales, but she has writer's block about how to choose one on her own. A bit of conversation with me is needed.

"Ella, do you remember what a lead is?" I ask.

"Yes. That's how you start your story off."

"Right you are," I say. "Have you thought of a lead for your bunny-and-dog fairy tale?"

"'Once upon a time,'" she answers without hesitating.

"Good choice," I say.

With beginning fiction writers, familiar storybook language is often the way to go. It is standard and reliable. It teaches the elements. There will be plenty of time to branch off into original leads later in Ella's writing career. Right now, "Once upon a time" is perfect for her, and the tiny bit of hand-holding I do to help her realize the lead is time well spent.

Here's the cover and first page of Ella's final copy:

The Magic Bunny and the
Bad Dog

by Ella Dempsey-Blair

Once upon a time there lived a bunny.

-1-

Cover and first page of Ella's book, *The Magic Bunny and the Bad Dog*

For a full-color version of this child's work, please see the website, books.heinemann.com/demille

Ella is a newcomer to writing fiction, but it is clear she knows plenty about the structure. Because she has already drawn pictures of her main characters and setting, she is able to write and draw this part of her book independently.

She clearly shows the main characters on the front cover of her book, following the example of many favorite authors she has read. On the first page she uses the traditional "Once upon a time" lead to begin her fairy tale and introduces the main character, the bunny. Although she initially withholds the information that this is a magic bunny, she foreshadows the bunny's powers by drawing it with magic wings. The bunny is also smiling. The careful picture tells all we need to know about the bunny at this point in the story.

One page 2, Ella provides important character description, revealing that the bunny is magic. Her drawing shows him flying over the red landscape of Candyland, grasping his huge magic

He was magic.

He lived in Candyland.

-2-

-3-

Pages 2 and 3 of Ella's book

wand. On page 3, she fulfills the requirement to tell about the setting, showing us the bunny's house and disclosing the location.

Let's recap. Ella has introduced the main character and setting. She has described her main character. With these elements of fiction in place, she is ready to move on to introduce and describe the opposing character, but she is now at a loss about how to do so. She again comes to me for help.

I look at her brilliant drawing of the magic bunny with the magic wand on page 3, put the book down in front of her, and ask, "Ella, what does the bunny have that the dog might want?"

"The wand!" she says.

"Why does he want the wand?" I ask, with no idea what the answer will be.

"He's jealous of the bunny because the bunny has magic."

"Do you want to put that in your book?" I ask.

"Yes," she replies.

A bad dog lived in Candyland. He was a robber. He was jealous of the bunny. He wanted the magic wand.

-4-

One night the bunny fell asleep. The dog stole the wand.

-5-

Ella's book *(continued)*

With that bit of help, Ella introduces the bad dog on page 4. She gets right to the point. She tells the reader three important details to vilify him: he is bad, he is a robber, and he has a character flaw. Every evil fairy tale character has a flaw, usually one of the seven deadly sins—jealousy, vanity, gluttony, greed, extravagance, sloth, or pride. The dog fits right in. He is jealous of the wand and wants it. That's as deep as Ella goes, but at her level of development, it's perfect.

During our most recent conference, I didn't offer any help beyond what Ella asked for. To move on to the next page before she had finished what she was working on would have overwhelmed her with information. Instead, I responded element by element, question by question. (Something that took place when I was teaching kindergarten underscores the wisdom of this approach. A boy asked me where he had come from, and instead of launching into how babies are made, I asked, "What do you mean?" He said, "Was it Philadelphia or Pittsburgh?")

I wonder whether Ella will be back to speak to me about how the dog will get the wand. And indeed, now that her characters have been set, and she has revealed what the opposing character wants, she shows up for more help.

"I'm stuck."

"How are you stuck?"

"I don't know."

"Show me where you are in your story, please."

She is facing the next blank page—intimidating for a writer of any age. I look at the preceding picture of the dog with the money bag and what she has written about his wanting the wand.

"It looks like we know your characters and your setting really well. You said that the dog wants the bunny's magic wand, right?"

"Yes."

"How is he going to get it from the bunny?" I ask.

"He could wait until the bunny goes to sleep and steal it," she answers.

"That is a great idea, Ella. So, do you want to put that in?"

"I will," she says, and off she goes. I fully expect her to pop back up at my elbow when she gets to the next page.

Ella springs the story problem on page 5. In the picture, the stealthy dog takes advantage of an opportunity and steals the wand while the magic bunny sleeps. Ella personifies the bunny by depicting him sleeping in a bed, while the dog "tip-paws" out the front door with the wand in his mouth. He's gotten what he wants.

That section completed, Ella comes knocking at my virtual door, once more looking stuck. She's looking for help with her rising action, problem solution, and satisfying ending. In fiction, these three elements follow in close and connected progression, so they are easy to discuss and plan in a single chunk. I decide to try that. Since she has responded immediately and appropriately to our discussions about the other elements, I figure she is ready for a bigger challenge.

"How can I help you, Ella?" I ask.

"I can't think of what to write."

"So you need help deciding what to write for the last part of your story?" I sum up.

"Yes."

"OK. We can do that. Let's see if we can make a plan that will help you finish your story right to the very end. Right now the bad dog has the magic wand, right?"

"Yes."

"So your bunny is still asleep?"

"No, he waked up and is sad . . . no, angry that the wand is gone."

"I get it. Your bunny wakes up and is angry that the wand is gone. Do you want to write that down?"

"Yes," she says and records the words in approximate spelling on her draft.

When she has finished, I ask, "Can I ask you another question about your story, or will that be confusing?"

"No, go ahead."

"I can tell the bunny has woken up now and that he is mad the wand is gone. Does he know the dog took the wand?"

"No."

"How is the bunny going to find out that the dog took the wand?" (When conferring, my favorite questions about story content are the questions I don't know the answers to. I love responding as an interested audience. That's easy when the stories are this compelling.)

Ella thinks a minute, and I can almost see the lightbulb appear above her head.

"He sees the dog tracks! I know how to draw really good doggy tracks!" she says with wide eyes and waving arms.

"Write that down!" I suggest, catching her excitement.

She records the words on her draft. As she gets to the last few letters, I decided to press a little further.

"Ella, now I know how the bunny can tell who took the wand. Can you tell me how the bunny is going to find the dog so he can get his wand back?"

The look on her face tells me she is rolling with it now. "He can follow the tracks and he can take the wand back when the dog isn't looking," she says. Then before I can respond, she adds, "And he'll be sorry and learn a lesson and never do it again."

When I ask, "He'll never do what again?" I expect her to say, "Steal the wand," but she surprises me in a delightful way.

"Anything mean."

"That all sounds great, Ella. Can you write that down?"

And she follows through.

The bunny woke up! He was angry because his wand was gone.

-6-

He saw dog footprints. He knew the dog took the wand.

-7-

Ella's story *(continued)*

On pages 6 and 7, the problem is revealed, but not explicitly stated. On page 6, the bunny is angry that his wand is gone. He has moved outdoors now and stands in front of his candy house, gazing into the distance with a frowning face. On page 7, he finds the dog tracks and knows who took the wand. Ella has created palpable tension here: we aren't sure what the dog is going to do, so we turn the page to find out.

On page 8, Ella has the bunny follow the tracks all the way to the dog's hut, and on page 9, the bunny gets back the wand while the dog isn't looking. There isn't a violent confrontation or an exchange of dialogue, just the restoration of harmony. The story problem is solved.

On the tenth and final page, Ella ends the story with the bad dog learning a lesson.

The dog is contrite. He feels bad about having taken what didn't

He followed the footprints to the dog's house.

While the dog wasn't looking he took the wand.

-8-

-9-

Ella's story *(continued)*

belong to him. That is enough in Ella's world. In the grand tradition of the fairy tale, Ella has left us with a moral: crime doesn't pay.

Ella was able to weave a charming cautionary tale for her classroom community and the wider world. With my support, she grappled with each of the distinct elements of fiction, asked for help when she needed it, came up with interesting and original ideas, and executed them. The result was a focused, organized, and compelling original piece of literature.

This is an enormous achievement for a young writer. Ella will build on this experience to write more fiction as she grows. Along the way she'll continue to receive help when and where she needs it. Soon she'll be a more fully independent writer solving increasingly more complex writing problems.

The dog learned a lesson and never did anything mean again.

-10-

Ella's conclusion

8 CHAPTER

Max Writes a Sophisticated Fairy Tale

*L*et's complete our investigation of fairy tales with a close reading of one written by midyear second grader Max. Max has had considerable experience reading and writing fiction. This year he has become interested in futuristic spy books that feature characters getting themselves in and out of tricky jams and barely escaping from dangerous situations. He has written in the style of Seuss, Henkes, Lobel, and Joy Cowley.

Max is a talented storyteller. He has written numerous memoirs and family stories, including a riveting true-life action tale documenting his father's rescue from a distressed yacht foundering in a storm in the Atlantic Ocean. Max is an avid and independent reader, an athlete, and a good friend and companion to his classmates. Perhaps Max's greatest passion is his love for machines and all things electronic. He is my favorite person to visit an electronics store with.

Max's fairy tale is titled *I Love Dragons*. The surprising and unique element of this work is that the story features a female main character who tells the entire story from her point of view. First-person narration in a primary-grade story is rare. It is even rarer for a boy to write in the voice of a girl. Let's look at *I Love Dragons* page by page.

I Love Dragons

by Max Burtis

Cover of *I Love Dragons*

For a full-color version
of this child's work,
please see the website,
books.heinemann.com/demille

The front cover of Max's booklet features the story's fearsome dragon villain. Max uses skills developed from drawing numerous dinosaurs and lizards in creating this detailed dragon. For the background sky, he attempts cross-hatching, a technique the class noticed in Maurice Sendak's and Arnold Lobel's books, to create and enhance shadows.

Hi, I'm Ashley and I love dragons.
I'm going to tell you a story of the time I
got a book from my Uncle Ralph. I
liked it because it was all about
dragons!

-1-

Max's lead

Max begins his story with a chatty, effective lead. He chooses a conversational tone similar to that used in fairy tales I've read aloud and that he remembers from reading the Zack Files series, by Dan Greenberg, and the My Weird School books, by Dan Gutman. Both series are told in first person, like kid versions of Raymond Chandler novels. Max has the main character, Ashley, introduce herself and the book within the book that is the vehicle for the main plot.

It was a magic book. When I opened
it to the page about dragon myths ... the
book took me to a magic land.

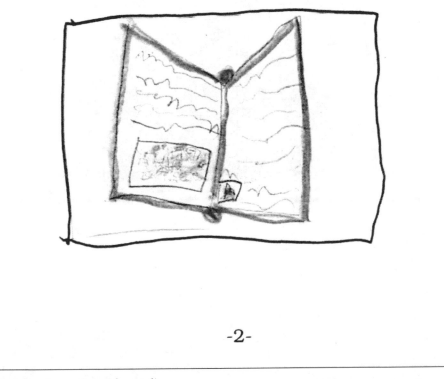

-2-

Max's story *(continued)*

On Max's second page, Ashley reveals the power of the book and talks about where it took her when she opened it to a particular page. Max remembers and borrows this device from Mary Pope Osborne's Magic Tree House series, which he read, in chronological order, during first grade. In the grand tradition of *A Connecticut Yankee in King Arthur's Court*, *The Wizard of Oz*, *The Lion, the Witch, and the Wardrobe*, and countless other stories, Max is employing the magic of teleporting.

The bad thing about it was that I
was locked into a high tower, and there
was a dragon guarding it...

-3-

Max's story *(continued)*

Max balances the joy of being transported to another time and place with the sorrow of being locked in a high tower guarded by a dragon. The high tower could be borrowed from Rapunzel, but I also read aloud Anna Quinlan's short novel *Happily Ever After* to the class last year. This story, with its brilliant illustrations by James Stevenson, chronicles a primary-age girl's journey back to medieval times courtesy of a magic baseball mitt. Max (consciously or not) has dipped back into his memory and used information stored there to write a similar scene for his book.

The illustration on page 3 is also worth discussing, because Max has pulled back his point of view to show a panorama of the entire castle, with the huge, lumbering dragon (dwarfing the castle and the tower) standing guard. In film this would be called an establishing shot. It introduces both the setting and the opposing character very effectively.

So I was stuck in the tower. Oh yeah, I was dressed in cool princess clothes. And how can I describe the tower? It had a bench, a big bowl, and a mesh window with an old fashioned latch. So the problem is that I was locked into the tower with a dragon guarding it. But then a weird looking prince showed up. He said, "Hello, I have come to...um..uh...free you!" I felt great. Then I saw the dragon. I yelled, "Watch out for the dragon!"

-4-

Max's story *(continued)*

Page 4 is all text. Max is becoming quite comfortable with print and needs fewer pictures to tell his story. He has mastered the art of description to the degree that he feels comfortable painting pictures with words.

Max brings real voice to his main character, writing dialogue that captures the way he has heard girls his age talk. Ashley gives us a good look at the inside of the tower and foreshadows how her first problem, imprisonment, will be solved.

In my experience (and at the risk of alienating all the females reading this book), had a girl been writing this, there probably would have been more description of the princess' clothes and more focus on how the character looked. Max moves the story along by describing the setting and introducing a new character: the prince. *Weird* is Max's default descriptor. He uses it to describe everything from food to his younger brother's behavior to how he feels about any given subject. It pops up here in his story, perhaps to characterize the prince as unconfident or hapless.

The action heats up as Ashley sees the dragon react to the prince's arrival and shouts out a warning. Max uses a cliff-hanger at the end of this page—what's going to happen?—a genuine page-turning moment. We care about what happens to Ashley and the prince because of the choices Max has made, the engaging way he has told the story. He's done this without sharing any pictures of the princess or the prince. We have seen only the setting and the fearsome dragon. Ashley's words and the confident way she talks make us root for her. We root for the prince because of his good intentions and because he seems to be in real danger from the dragon.

On page 5 Max chooses to provide detailed description. In Ashley's voice, he uses five complete sentences to tell about all aspects of the dragon and confirm that the prince is facing a formidable opponent. The illustration works in perfect concert with the words. The prince looks completely overmatched against the cold castle walls with the fireball raining down on him and the dragon's teeth and claws within striking distance.

Max makes an interesting and effective choice on page 6. After it's clear that the fireball has missed the prince, Max diffuses the tension with two slapstick moments sandwiching an amusing judgment by his main character. (Max has already used slapstick humor in his Lobel-style story and constantly jokes and laughs with his friends about this type of comedy.) First the prince falls down. Then Ashley repeats her earlier assessment that he is weird, meaning helpless or in need of assistance. This statement is followed immediately by the prince's visor falling down over his eyes,

Suddenly, the dragon turned around! The dragon was covered with pickle green scales. Big red plates ran down his back. His claws were as sharp as nails. His eyes glowed like hot coals. He had razor sharp teeth and two fangs in front that touched. He heaved a big fireball at the prince.

-5-

Max's story *(continued)*

The weird prince ducked, then fell down. "Man that prince is weird," I said to myself. The prince got up and started fighting. Suddenly, his visor plopped down over his eyes.

-6-

Max's story *(continued)*

a moment borrowed from another source, *Time Cat*, by Lloyd Alexander. In that book a boy and a cat visit Peru during the time of the Incas. Another character is forced against his will to be a soldier and has all kinds of difficulty with his armor, one being that the visor on his helmet constantly falls down.

In the accompanying illustration, Max draws a close-up of the prince's head so we focus on the falling visor. The illustration shows how helpless the prince is when trapped inside the helmet—not able to see, the dragon breathing down his neck. We

Then the prince started swinging his sword violently, in all directions. Then I thought, "He's going to get himself killed." So I opened the latch on the window. I took the big bowl and threw it out the mesh window at the dragon.

-7-

Max's story *(continued)*

know the prince is still in trouble and expect another immediate attack.

On page 7 Max has Ashley step in and assist the prince before the unthinkable happens. As the prince swings wildly at the dragon, she attempts to save him by unlatching the window and heaving a bowl toward the dragon. Max shows us a close-up of the prince again and uses cartoony movement lines to indicate a violently swinging sword. He also gives us another page-turning moment by waiting to reveal the outcome of the bowl toss until the next page.

The bowl hit the dragon on the head and knocked him out. When the prince finally got his visor up, his head was directly under the dragon's jaw!

-8-

Max's story *(continued)*

On page 8, the first of Ashley and the prince's problems is cleverly solved by Max's slapstick-comedy device of the flying bowl. The prince gets his visor up and sees the danger he'd been in. This underscores how important it was for Ashley to take action and save the prince, who was originally there to save her.

Max keeps the prince in character—and maintains the steady stream of comedy—by having him faint from fright. He also

Once the prince noticed where he was, he quickly got out and fainted.

Now that I had saved the prince and knocked out the dragon, I had to think about getting out of the tower. I thought, man if I just had a … wait! I do have one! I grabbed a hairpin out of my hair and started picking the lock on the barred door.

-9-

Max's story *(continued)*

develops the ingenuity and self-sufficiency of his female protagonist by having her solve a second problem, thus making his tale a little more detailed and complicated. It is certainly in character for Max (who loves all things mechanical) to have Ashley attempt to pick the lock with a hairpin. Max is borrowing good ideas from the spy novels he's read by incorporating this escape scenario into his original fairy tale.

When I finally unlocked the barred
door, I ran down the tower steps.
Something fell out of my dress... it was
the magic book from Uncle Ralph! I
opened it to the page about dragon
myths and ... *nothing happened.*

-10-

Max's story *(continued)*

On page 10, Ashley begins her final escape, successfully open-
ing the tower door, descending the stairs, and recovering Uncle
Ralph's magic book from the folds of her dress. Max skillfully draws
out the ending, however, because the book fails to transport her
back to the present. The accompanying illustration uses a cartoon
question mark to indicate Ashley's confusion. Wondering if she will
ever get out of her fix, we turn eagerly to page 11.

Max brings the story to a short and sweet conclusion. He solves
Ashley's exit from danger by having her turn to another page in the

Then I had an idea, I opened it to the page about different dragons teleporting themselves to different places and times. Next thing I knew, I was back in my room living happily ever after!

-11-

Max's conclusion

book about teleporting, which does send her back home. He ends the story by charmingly working the classic fairy tale "happily ever after" into Ashley's informal way of speaking.

Max has accomplished something remarkable in writing and illustrating his original fairy tale. He's included his own interests in and knowledge of magic, technology of the future, machines, and action-adventure fiction. He's written about what he knows and loves, having learned that he can write with authority and authenticity about subjects about which he is passionate.

Max has included all the elements of fiction in this tale—a chatty and effective lead, an engaging introduction of the main character, a clear description (particularly in connection with his illustration) of the setting, a detailed written description of the opposing character, two clever problems, funny and dramatic solutions, and a quick and satisfying happy ending. Along the way, he has used considerable skill in drawing out the action and breaking up tense moments with humor. Because of this increased dramatic tension, the story resolutions are all the more satisfying.

Max, like all the authors (famous and unknown) who precede him, has borrowed ideas and plot devices from favorite books that he judged would be useful and effective in his original story. The teleporting-book device from Mary Pope Osborne, the hapless prince from Anna Quinlan, and the visor drop from Lloyd Alexander are all affectionate homages to authors Max respects and loves.

Max has made a courageous choice to write from the perspective of a young girl. Neither I nor anyone I've talked to who teaches writing to primary children would label this a common occurrence. Indeed, few remember it ever happening. He has also chosen to write his book in the first person, another brave and seldom-attempted feat in fiction written by young children. He succeeds admirably on both fronts.

There are parts of the story that probably could have been further revised and edited. However, to do so would have risked removing the wonderful, charming, and effective voice of a young writer attempting original fiction.

In this story Max shows he has a firm grasp and understanding of the elements of fiction. He can now independently compose fiction in school and at home. He has joined the ranks of Henkes, Lobel, and all the other authors he knows and loves. He and his classmates can consider themselves part of a community of fiction writers committed to developing growing skills and strategies in storytelling and illustrating. They are a tribe of writers who know how to identify and read quality fiction, can unpack a story to see just how the author accomplished writing a great book. Most important, Max and his classmates understand the purpose of writing fiction: to make believe on paper, have a blast doing it, and provide their family, friends, and the public at large with good stories that can be enjoyed forever after.

As you've seen, fiction is a viable and necessary genre for primary school students to study and create. Here are a few words of friendly advice as you start (or continue) to help them do so:

- *Start slowly.* When my class is studying fiction, we don't always do everything I've talked about in this book. I pick and choose, depending on the circumstances and the students in each class. The writing arc is long, and there are many other important genres to cover. So pace yourself, especially if you are making a place for fiction writing in your classroom for the first time. One author study and one fairy tale make a great beginning.

- *Watch and listen to what children do naturally.* I got the idea to teach my first and second graders how to write stories from observing them at play, during lunch, and during free time. I noticed them acting out and talking about their own make-believe adventures, and then stapling paper together in order to write them down. Observing children when they don't know they are being watched and paying attention to the stories they are spinning on their own are invaluable ways to collect information that will help you make every one of your students a better writer.

- *Meet children where they are and challenge them from there.* Children will enter your classroom with a wide range of skills, strategies, interests, and expertise. Some will be able to tell good stories right from the start. Some will be talented picture makers. Others will be able to record sounds on paper easily and efficiently. Meet them where they are and build bridges from there to each story-writing skill. If you are fortunate enough to be able to work with children for a number of years, you'll be able to watch these connections happen. The progression from oral storytelling to drawing to writing is powerful, and all three skills are vital to creating quality fiction.

- *Embrace and extend off-the-page storytelling experiences.* Reading quality literature aloud, encouraging children to read independently and giving them time to do so, teaching them how to notice what an author is doing and why, teaching them how to draw a picture to help them describe a character or a setting, and introducing them to story-planning sheets are all worthwhile ways to help your students become better fiction writers.

- *Demonstrate with your own writing.* Try this stuff out yourself. You need only a little more expertise than your students at the beginning of the year. Primary school students are a most accepting audience. By demonstrating with your own writing, you show children that you are struggling with the same problems. You also gain a little more compassion for the developing writer.

- *Listen to and talk with your students.* Encourage and cultivate discussion of all types of fiction. Allow your children to introduce topics important to them. Investigate and show an interest in their personal knowledge, individual histories, loves, collections, hobbies, and obsessions. Share this same information about yourself. You'll unearth a plethora of potential topics for stories and build a stronger relationship with each and every student.

A few days before I finished this book, I spent a few minutes talking with Josie's mother, Sally, when she came to pick her daughter up after school. Sally told me that Josie was enjoying studying fiction and had begun to write stories at home about her riding lessons. In these stories, the main character, also named Josie, had adventures featuring some of the horses at the riding stable. I was intrigued and asked Josie if she would bring the stories in.

"Well," she said, "it's a chapter book. I only have one chapter done."

"Can you bring that chapter in? I'd love to see it," I said.

"OK."

The next day Josie brought in a table of contents and her first chapter. The table of contents listed eleven chapters dealing with a full range of topics. In the first (two-page) chapter, which included an illustration, the main character, Josie, courageously ropes a runaway horse. (Those three pages and their translations are reproduced on the following pages.)

The goal of education in general, and any writing program in particular, is to help students gain independence. Josie had found a place for writing in her life. It was a vehicle she used to express her dream of being a roping cowgirl and a competent horsewoman.

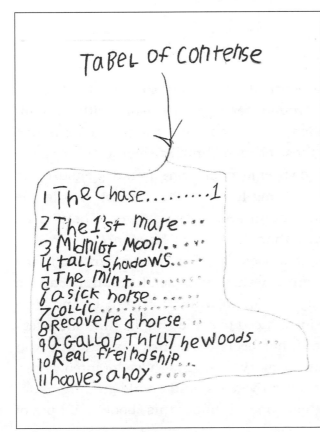

Table of Contents

Up she went! Mane and tail thrashing—she flew over the log. Riley galloped after Zan, Josie riding on Riley, nobody riding on Zan.

Josie had a rope. Well, she divided the rope in half, so it made a loop. Then she took one end of the rope and pulled it through the loop. It made a perfect cowgirl loop—but now it was going to be used as a horse-catching loop.

She had no time to waste, she threw the loop around Zan's neck. She slowed Riley to a trot. Then a walk. Then halted and tied Riley to a tree. Zan hung her head, knowing she had been caught. Josie untied Riley and hopped on and she trotted Zan back to the stable.

> 1
>
> The chase
>
> upshe went! Mane and Tail Thrashing she flew over The log. Riley Galloped after san.Josie rideing oh Riley nobody Rideing on san.Josie had a rope. well ropio she dewded The rope in haf so it made a loop Thensheh took Loop, it Made a perfect cowgirl it Thew The used as a cow caching Loop—but That was Going to be used as a horse cathcing loop.
>
> she had no time to waset she Threw The loop around sans neck she slowed Riley to a trot,Then a walk Then halted and tide riley to a tree. san hung her head knowing Thatshe had been caut.Josie untide Riley and hoped oh.and she trotted san back to The staBel.

She took the lessons she learned about how to write fiction, the information she gained through her apprenticeship with brilliant authors, the skill she honed as an artist, and the passion she had for horses and combined these elements into authentic and original literature created for her own enjoyment. She found pleasure not only in having written something for an audience but also in the acts of writing and illustrating in and of themselves. There is no greater reward for a teacher than seeing that happen.

Thank you for reading this book. The best part of writing it has been having the opportunity to show you what children can do when they are given plenty of time in which to listen to and read quality literature and are introduced to some simple, fun, and effective ways of writing fiction. It has been a pleasure to share with you the wonderful stories my primary students have created. Now, under your watchful eyes, attentive ears, and gentle guiding hand, your children can do the same. I hope this book will be of

Josie dismounted and she gave Riley a horse cookie, and Zan a mint. Riley was greedy when you gave him mints so Josie gave him a horse cookie. Josie untacked Riley and put Zan and him in the correct stable. Josie groomed them and brushed their manes and tails.

assistance as you shepherd your students' forays into the exciting world of writing fiction. I wish you luck as you work and learn together to discover the possibilities, challenges, and achievements of writing this important, necessary, and inspiring genre. Have fun making believe on paper.

Bettelheim, Bruno. 1976. *The Uses of Enchantment: The Meaning and Importance of Fairy Tales*. New York: Knopf.

Commission on Reading. 1985. *Becoming a Nation of Readers*. http://www.readaloudamerica.org/about.htm

Harwayne, Shelley. 2003. Lecture at Walloon Institute.

Henkes, Kevin. 2007. *A Good Day*. New York: Greenwillow/HarperCollins.

Henkes, Kevin. 2008. HarperCollins.com. HarperCollins author webpages. www.kevinhenkes.com

Horn, Martha, and Mary Ellen Giacobbe. 2007. *Talking, Drawing, Writing: Lessons for Our Youngest Writers*. York, ME: Stenhouse.

Lobel, Arnold. 1972. *Mouse Tales*. New York: HarperTrophy.

Pitcher, Evelyn Goodenough, and Ernst Prelinger. 1963. *Children Tell Stories: An Analysis of Fantasy*. New York: International Universities Press.

Prescott, Orville. 1965. *A Father Reads to His Children*. 1965. New York: Dutton.

Trelease, Jim. 2006. *The Read-Aloud Handbook*. 6th ed. New York: Penguin Books.

Wikipedia contributors. 2008. "Children's Literature." *Wikipedia, the Free Encyclopedia*. en.wikipedia.org/w/index.php?title=Children%27s_literature&oldid=211077757 (accessed 2008).